ROUND PEG, SQUARE HOLE

ROUND PEG, SQUARE HOLE

A TEACHER LIVES AND LEARNS IN WATTS

John Gust

Foreword by Ron Miller

HEINEMANN
Portsmouth, NH

Heinemann
A division of Reed Elsevier Inc.
361 Hanover Street
Portsmouth, NH 03801–3912
http://www.heinemann.com

Offices and agents throughout the world

Library of Congress Cataloging-in-Publication Data

Gust, John
Round peg, square hole: a teacher lives and learns in Watts/John Gust: foreword by Ron Miller: [editor, Lois Bridges].
p. cm.
Includes bibliographical references.
ISBN 0-325-00090-5 (alk. paper)
1. Minorities—Education (Elementary)—California—Los Angeles—Case studies. 2. Gust, John 3. Elementary school teachers—California—Los Angeles—Biography. 4. Watts (Los Angeles, Calif.)—Social conditions. I. Bird, Lois Bridges. II. Title.
LC3725.G87 1999
372.11'0092—dc21 98-52710
CIP

Editor: Lois Bridges
Production: Vicki Kasabian
Cover design: Darci Mehall/Aureo Design
Manufacturing: Louise Richardson

Printed in the United States of America on acid-free paper

03 DA 2 3 4 5

This book is dedicated to those teachers who oftentimes find their values, beliefs, and philosophies regarding schooling at odds with the public education system. My greatest hope is that this book will provide some small measure of encouragement for them to carry on, to follow their beliefs and their heart for the benefit of the wonderful children they teach.

Contents

Foreword

Ron Miller

It is not fashionable to practice education, much less write about it, as a passionate and meaning-laden encounter between human beings. As a society, we rarely think about education as a means for nourishing our children's lives, inspiring their dreams, or initiating them into a wondrous world or even a meaningful culture. In the mass media, in the paltry education sections of most bookstores, and in the draconian educational policies of national and state governments, *schooling* is defined as a task of social engineering, turning out as its "product" masses of people who can process information and perform work in the global corporate economy. In this age of decadent materialism, few of us seem concerned about enriching young people's lives, or inviting them to experience meaning, wonder, or joy—there is, instead, a monotonous insistence on "accountability" and "standards," as if mechanizing our children's minds will somehow bring about a society in which it is worth living.

About thirty years ago, a generation rebelled against the drudgery, meaninglessness, and standardization of modern schooling. Thousands, indeed hundreds of thousands, of people read the angry, passionate, visionary books of educators such as A. S. Neill, John Holt, George Dennison, Jonathan Kozol, Herbert Kohl, and James Herndon. Many of these books were issued by some of the leading publishing houses in the nation and reviewed in important periodicals. For a few years, between the late 1960s and mid-1970s, it looked as though an educational revolution might be brewing, as policymakers, foundations, universities, and educational leaders tried radical ideas in schools, such as open classrooms, alternative programs, off-campus learning, and various techniques for enhancing learning and holistic personal development. In hindsight, we can recognize that many of these reforms were naïve and superficial, but we must never forget that they were motivated by a sincere and passionate belief that *people's lives matter*, that our personhood and individuality must count more than raw economic interests. Today our culture is being consumed by these latter interests, and as a result, our educational policies are dreary and deadening.

John Gust is a passionate and idealistic educator who has rediscovered what the educational visionaries of that generation tried to tell us. Like George Dennison's marvelous account of his life-giving school in the inner city, *Round Peg, Square Hole* is concerned about *the lives of children*—the quality and texture and meaning of their lives, not solely their employment prospects. Gust argues, and amply demonstrates, that if we truly care about young people and the communities in which they live, then education must come from the heart and soul, not merely from techniques or standards. Gust tells us why he found conventional schooling routines inadequate to the educational needs of his students, and then tells an inspiring story about his search for a more meaningful way of teaching, to which, in the face of resistance, doubt, and fear, he dedicated himself wholeheartedly.

This author belongs to a dissenting tradition in American education that has variously been called "progressive," "alternative," and "holistic." Educators in this tradition do not accept the dominant cultural, political, and intellectual views of schooling as an agency of social discipline and conformity; rather, they attempt to call forth the diverse creative energies of young people themselves. Such educators have often been ridiculed as "romantic" by those who value efficiency and control, but why is it "romantic" to point out the verifiable fact that standardized, autocratic learning environments carry significant educational and developmental costs? Gust, like earlier dissident educators, observes that most young people do not thrive in classrooms that ignore their real needs and channel their life energies into dull routines. There is nothing sentimental about providing a more authentic and democratic community that invites rather than hinders active participation, critical inquiry, and collaborative action. This is a strong moral and political act, as progressive educators from Dewey and Counts to Jonathan Kozol and Herbert Kohl to Paulo Freire and contemporary critical theorists have all recognized. Gust belongs to this tradition, yet his writing is not as angry or abstract as many of theirs. He simply testifies that canned, legislated, coerced learning does not inspire his kids to strive or achieve, and that democratic participation and human engagement in fact have the power to inspire genuine learning.

Gust began his quest with some wrenching, searching questions. "Is life nothing more than personal survival in a meaningless and unfriendly world?" he asked. "Did education have to be so trite and mundane? . . . Did we just want to produce mindless, unquestioning citizens that were incapable of thinking critically about what was happening in the world? . . . Was our sole purpose just to consume?" He wondered why so few educators pause to ask such questions, or any questions about the philosophy or purpose of schooling. And then, in fine Deweyan form, he *acted* upon the results of his questioning. For starters, he recognized that in order to address the racial tensions he experienced as a white teacher in a largely segregated Latino and African American school, he would need to "quit talking and writing about the problem and actually take individual responsibility and do something about it!" So he moved from his own comfortable neighborhood into Watts, and became involved in the lives of his students and neighbors in a way that few educators dare. Like Kozol in *Death at an Early Age,* Gust was warned that he could not be an effective (i.e., authoritative) teacher if he was also a friend to his students, but he recognized that this advice was based on faulty premises about the nature of teaching, and so he wisely ignored it.

The point of this book, as I see it, is that progressive education, a person-centered, meaning-centered education, actually transforms people's lives. It gives young people wider horizons in which to aspire and strive, empowers them to dream and achieve in ways they couldn't previously imagine. This is our highest calling as educators, and we betray our calling when we become entranced by curriculum, test scores, and standards.

I wish the politicians and technocrats dictating educational policy today would read this book, and understand what damage they are doing to young people and to our culture by pursuing their misguided crusade for standardization. John Gust clearly shows us that human caring and engagement, not standards, are the vital essence of genuine education.

Ron Miller was founding editor of the journal Holistic Education Review *and is the author of* What Are Schools For? Holistic Education in American Culture.

Acknowledgments

Without a doubt the experiences that have led to the writing of this book have been by far the most trying and challenging of my life. So many extraordinary people have contributed to make this experience and resulting book possible. To each of you I would like to extend my heartfelt thanks.

First and foremost, to Meghan McChesney: Your friendship, encouragement, and interest has helped me time and time again to see the value in all of what *we* have done. During those times when I was extremely discouraged, your relentless supply of strength, support, and wisdom helped me to carry on. Thanks for being there.

To Georges Goulet: Whether you are aware of it or not, it was actually you who inspired me to move into the Watts community. In so doing, I was only hoping to become half the educator that you are. I thoroughly enjoyed all of our numerous philosophic discussions and much-needed counseling sessions. And I'd like to thank you once again for all your valuable contributions to the field of education and systems design.

To Ron Miller: Thanks, Ron, for perusing the original manuscript and suggesting that I send it to Lois Bridges at Heinemann. Thanks also for all of your inspiring work in the field of holistic education. I hope that you can recognize the influence of your work reflected in the pages here.

To Lois Bridges, my editor at Heinemann: Because of the benefit of your teaching, I learned more about myself as a writer, educator, and human being. Thank you for all the words of encouragement and insightful suggestions.

To the 4-H organization, and especially to John, Deirdre, and Don: Thank you for the opportunity to involve the children in 4-H program in the design and beautification of the Hacienda Village playground.

To Victor Cole, one of the most powerful people I have ever known: Thank you for welcoming me to the community, for all of your guidance, advice, and protection. Most of all, thank you for being a friend.

To Mr. Watkins: Thank you for all the supportive "get real" talks that we had on your front porch. I only wish that more people could learn, as I did, from the example that you and your wonderful, exemplary family provide. I agree, sir, you truly are blessed . . . as I have been, from your presence.

And most important, I would like to thank my friends: the children. By far the most valuable learning that I have ever received came from simply being in your company. I am so very grateful that all of you—my students and other friends from the neighborhood—have allowed me in your life.

Reluctant Return

The night before my interview at Compton Avenue Elementary School in Watts, I decided to take a drive to check out the neighborhood. Check out the neighborhood!? Watts!? The infamous inner-city home of riots, gangs, drive-by shootings, poverty, and crime? Yep, that was the place.

Before making my decision, however, I spent a lot of time thinking about it in my apartment-with-a-view in upscale, breezy Manhattan Beach. Why did I want to go? Why now? It was nearly 10 PM! What was eating at me? What was I hoping to find? I could get shot at. I could get . . .

Preparing to leave, I became aware of how scared I was. My hands were actually shaking. In an attempt to calm my mounting fear with something to eat, I looked in the cabinet, spied a bag of Frito's, grabbed it, then turned to the fridge and snatched a 7-Up. Munchies in hand, I made my way to the sliding glass door, closed it, and without stopping to lock up, scurried off to my Jeep. After jumping in and slamming the door, I started to have second thoughts. But to prevent myself from changing my mind, I quickly pulled out of the parking space and drove to the freeway as fast as possible.

Driving east on the newly constructed 105 freeway, I began daydreaming. Flashbacks from the last five years screamed through my head. After resigning from the Los Angeles Unified School District (LAUSD) two years ago, I swore I'd never go back. And I still did not, under any circumstances, want to go back. When I quit, I collected my retirement pay—with a penalty of course—and ran as fast as I could. I told myself that I would never go back into the classroom—at least not a classroom controlled by the directives of another large bureaucratic school system.

When I left the school district, teachers were about to receive a ten percent pay cut. A ten percent pay cut!? Did the administration think that I was going to just lay down and take a ten percent pay cut after all I did for the district, my school and students. I poured my heart and soul into teaching for three good, solid years. They had to be kidding! The administration wasn't proposing a ten percent reduction in time and dedication. My attitude was, "Screw it, I'm history."

The consummate overachiever, I worked my tail off those three years. In addition to my regular classroom assignment—which was more than enough in itself—I started an after-school fun and fitness program which met two days per week for two hours each day; out of my own pocket I paid for a mural my fifth grade class painted on one of the walls at our school (plus I constantly repainted the mural every Monday morning after the "taggers" marred it over the weekend); I brought in volunteers for a schoolwide exercise assembly; I brought in a special acrobatic team for the school to watch at an outdoor assembly on the playground; I gave a number of workshops on how to enhance students' self-esteem; and I participated in countless extra school assignments and duties. I had worked nonstop in my classroom, for my school, for the district and surrounding community. And how was the district showing its appreciation? By rewarding me with a ten percent pay cut! I should have been getting a raise. I was gone! Good-bye, so long, adios!

You could say that I was just another burnt-out used-to-be-ambitious teacher who left the public school system due to the all too common reasons: low pay, lack of respect, few opportunities for advancement, lack of administrative support, unnecessary bureaucratic demands, poorly maintained buildings, excessive nonteaching duties, lack of parental involvement, limited autonomy, isolation from other teachers, and a lack of a voice in governance and decision making. But that wouldn't be completely accurate. For some reason, something else about what we were doing in school bothered me. Something else that I couldn't quite put my finger on.

I was able to stay out of the classroom for two years working as an educational consultant while also acquiring a masters' degree. I presented seminars at a number of educational conferences and schools, wrote a few teacher resource books, and was commissioned by a company that manufactured and marketed various educational products to facilitate a research project that assessed the effectiveness of a beginning reading program.

Unfortunately, in spite of all my marketing efforts, eventually the work and my savings ran out. Defeated in my attempts to prosper as a consultant, I reluctantly returned, tail between my legs, to the Los Angeles Unified School District. And to put the icing on my recently acquired cake of defeat, the pay I was about to receive would be less that it was when I left the school system!

So there I was, driving into Watts, where I would probably end up working. I had taught in this area before, so I knew what I was getting into. In my prior years of teaching, I experienced the riots, the gang drive-by shootings, the fatherless children, the violence, the weekly graffiti, the constant threat of drugs, and the numerous school break-ins. But there I was again, getting right back in it. Could I honestly say that I wanted to go back? No. Could I tell you that I was going to like my job? Doubtful.

But I was going to be working with children! Sensitive, emotional children who were also angry, hurt, mean, happy, sad, warm, hard, loving, confused, lethargic, motivated, damaged, intelligent, honest, devious, creative, stubborn, flexible, carefree, scared, and brave. They were all of those things, and now they were going to have a teacher that really didn't want to be there and who most of the time, probably wouldn't like his job.

The outrageous thing about it was that the district, administration, and principal were dying to get me. They wouldn't admit it, but they were most likely dying to get just about any warm body (teacher shortages were rampant in most large under-resourced urban school districts), let alone an experienced, credentialed, master-degreed, author of teacher resource books, part-time educational consultant.

Yet, in spite of all of this, there I was, late at night, driving on the freeway, going to check out the neighborhood where I would probably be teaching. I had to be nuts.

By the time I approached the exit that would allow me to enter Watts, I had to stop. I could have kicked myself. I needed gas! What a fool. Why didn't I get gas before I left Manhattan Beach? How dumb could I be! Get gas in this neighborhood, at this hour? I didn't want to stop the Jeep, let alone get out of it. But I had no choice, so I pulled into the Shell station on the corner of Central and Imperial Highway. After parking the Jeep, I walked quickly to the cashier and handed him my five dollar bill through the bullet-proof glass.

When I went back to the Jeep to pump the gas, a Black man was already cleaning my windshield. I did not want anyone messing with my Jeep! The dirty-looking guy, with frayed clothes, also had the hose from the pump in my gas tank! I didn't much like that at all. He didn't ask for permission. He just forced his actions on me. And I knew he was going to expect something in return. But, he wasn't going to get anything, because I put all my money in the tank. I didn't want get stuck in Watts with any money in my pocket. No sir.

"How ya doin'?" I asked.

"Real good," he answered. "Sure is a beautiful night, don't ya think?" He obviously had no intention of explaining what he was doing, or how much he wanted.

"Yeah, I guess so," I said, waiting for him to put his hand out.

When all the gas was in the tank, he stood there and still without saying anything, looked at me for a moment. I looked back at him without saying a word. Finally, I said, "I just put all my money in the tank."

Then I opened my door, reached into my Jeep, held out what was left of my Frito's and said, "This is all I've got."

He shrugged his shoulders, said, "Better than nothin,' I guess," and snatched the bag from my hand. Walking away, he looked back over his shoulder and said, "Thanks."

Still scared, I jumped back in the Jeep and drove east on Imperial Highway toward Compton Avenue. The first street I passed was crowned Success Avenue. Success Avenue? Pretty ironic name for a street cutting through the Nickerson Gardens housing community, I thought. "Success Avenue"!? Around here?

Driving on, I reached the corner of Imperial and Compton Avenue. While idling in the left-hand turning lane, waiting for the light, I noticed the fenced-in, partially burnt remains of an abandoned Kentucky Fried Chicken restaurant. The asphalt lot looked like a polluted jungle covered with garbage and weeds gone wild.

As I turned the corner, the Jeep's headlights highlighted a spray-painted message on the side of the building. Slowing down to get good look, I read the big, black, bold capital letters.

> THE SYSTEM IS WAGING WAR ON THE PEOPLE
> THE PEOPLE MUST WAGE WAR ON I . . .

Whoever wrote the message obviously didn't get a chance to finish "IT". I chuckled when I imagined the small helpless writer being swallowed up by a huge monster of a "system" just as he was getting ready to complete his message. Driving on, I wondered which side I wanted to be on—the system's or the people's.

Shaking off the image, I continued driving north on Compton Avenue in what looked to be a Third World country. Of course, I had never been to a Third World country before, but as far as I was concerned this couldn't be far from it. Garbage was piled up everywhere! Abandoned buildings and cars, graffittied buildings, people pushing shopping carts, the carcass of a dead dog in the street, two stray dogs running by. The whole environment was gross, and it made my stomach turn.

By now it was after 10:30 and very dark. As I drove, my eyes continued to scan the road and sidewalks, looking for any sign of trouble. My knuckles were white from gripping the steering wheel so tightly. I was entirely ready to run over somebody if I had to. Nobody was going to come up to my Jeep, reach in, and take anything away from me. No way.

Eventually, I made it up Compton Avenue to 104th Street. The school was on the left, so I turned. Typical of most schools in Los Angeles, the entirely ashphalted grounds were surrounded by a tall chain-link fence. And, of course, all the classroom windows were protected by steel mesh coverings. Graffiti adorned some of the walls.

Still watching and waiting for someone to shoot at me, or a group of men to overtake the vehicle, I looked to my left. It was then that I saw two children, a boy and girl, pushing a smaller boy . . . in a red Radio Flyer wagon. They were on the sidewalk that bordered the Hacienda Village housing development, playing, laughing, having a wonderful time. I couldn't believe it. Here I was, shaking in my pants, totally ready to run over someone if I had to. What a fool I was. After seeing the kids, all I wanted to do was to get out of the Jeep so I could go play along. What did I have to be afraid of?

Classroom Essentials

After my interview the following morning, I was hired on, of course. Then, as expected, along with all my colleagues, I went through the rather arduous process of getting ready for my students: preparing my room, gathering materials, attending meetings and professional development workshops, and writing lessons and other essentials. By the first day of school, I was ready to teach.

Most teachers talk about how nervous they are on the first day of school. But not me, no sir. Heck, I reasoned, they're just a bunch of little kids; what could they do to make me so nervous? They're usually all nervous and on their very best behavior themselves the first day anyway. Kids always want to make a good first impression and please the teacher on the first day. Besides, whether we realize it or not, the kids are usually too busy looking the teacher over to see how competent, how friendly, how tough, how loving, and how organized they are.

Most people think of the elementary classroom as a very small place, but it's not really. As a true reflection of the collective consciousness of our time, it's actually large enough to house most of the good and bad of human nature. I think of it as a microcosm of some of the most humane acts and worst social problems of our time.

But, in my classroom, in spite of these myriad social problems and unrealized human potentials, the stipulated responsibility that our public school system assigned to all of us teachers was to basically keep one conservative goal in mind—the essentials. There was a lot of talk going around the district at the time about the pressure mounting to improve our students' test scores. The message was that our students' test scores had to improve, or else all the extra money that we were getting for our students' special needs would soon be lost. The test everyone was talking about, of course, was the California Test of Basic Skills—a test that teachers in our district had been administering to students for fifteen years. You'd think by now, after all these years of being exposed to the same test, that we educators would have figured out a way to help our students do well on this test. But such was not the case.

Compliantly doing just what was expected of me, I was to keep those kids in my classroom quiet, also compliant, and working to improve those test scores—regardless of anyone's belief otherwise, teaching to the test was the mode of the day. I disliked the accepted mainstream practices of our public school system. Hated being aware of what I was expected, required to do.

Throughout the year, I would be called on to administer not one, not two, but three practice or milepost tests at strategic intervals before the "real" standardized test was administered prior to summer break. And, of course, to make sure we would be on task, all of us teachers were also required to list on a poster all the specific, isolated, basic skill objectives that the upcoming milepost test would be addressing, and display it in some prominent place in the room.

So with all this pressure—perceived or actual—for my students to do well on the test, my charge was to present a multitude of lessons that would address specifically the types of items the students would encounter on the tests. Essentially speaking, as the authority in my classroom, it was my job to teach my students how to read, 'rite, and do 'rithmetic. I was supposed to transmit as much information, impart as much of our nation's established body of knowledge as possible into the passive and empty receptacles that were soon going to be entering my classroom.

In the authoritarian domain that accepted conventional practices fostered me to create, I was expected to know exactly where each child would sit. I was expected to know how, when, and where they would line up, when and where they would talk, raise their hands, sharpen their pencils, hang up their coats and bookbags, hand in their homework, recite the pledge, and go to the bathroom. Our daily schedule, ruled and objectified by the clock and the ceaseless sounding of bells, with its specific start and ending times for each isolated subject area, as expected, was also prominently displayed on the wall. As expected, student textbooks, journals, pencils, erasers, crayons, and scissors were all neatly arranged on the desks. And as commonly expected, my stacks of dittos were all ready, my teacher-directed lesson plans were all written, and my rules, rewards, and consequences were also posted in a proper place—my classroom's environmental stimuli and expected student responses were very clear.

In my classroom, and in our school, we had all the essentials. Because the prevailing thought was that no teacher could produce their lessons from scratch, we had every imaginable programmed, scripted, robotic, idiot-proofed, encyclopedia-sized instructional guide for every subject area you could think of. We had available to us every resource that helped children to improve their test-taking skills. And, of course, we had every possible publisher catalogue imaginable. But, not a single professional journal was to be found anywhere. All the information we were going to get about effective instructional practices, all the authoritative curriculum we were going to implement, came directly from the real determinants of curriculum—the publishers.

Primarily, we would stick with the basics, the isolated skills, the "repeat after me," "say the word, spell the word, say the word," "write the word, three times each," "fill in the blank," "copy the definition," overly pedantic, no-brainer stuff. In my classroom, we had an ambitious agenda. We would reach our educational goals for the year 2000! We were going to *act now* to educate America! We were going to measure up to the high standards set by some far-removed governing board. We were going to meet or exceed our national achievement test averages. Test scores would improve! Percentiles would go sky high!

Pick Up Your Feet!

James was the biggest and baddest dude in class—a kid with an attitude. He had that "I'm a tough guy!" look about him. He was the kind of kid that, when you looked at him, you *knew* was headed straight for the gangs, and trouble. His hair was always a mess, his clothes were always dirty, he hardly ever had his homework completed, and, when he was having a bad day, there was practically nothing you could do to bring him out of it. He didn't like to look any adult in the eye either.

I asked him one day why he wouldn't look me in the eye. He told me that if he did, people would yell at him, "Whatta you lookin' at?!" Maybe it had something to do with gangs, or maybe it was the kind of thing he heard at home, but I couldn't begin to think what that kind of talk would do to a child. Oh, he'd look me in the eye when I was far away, like when I was at the chalkboard and he was looking to answer a question, but when I talked directly with him in a nonreprimanding way, James never looked me in the eye.

Sometimes James could be a charmer with the girls though. Often I would see him joking and entertaining Leslie and Natasha to a point where he had them laughing, giggling, and practically eating out of his hands. They seemed to like his roughness and mostly quiet demeanor. Plus, he was a good looking boy, too. As far as his studies went, well, James had been going to the reading specialist for about two years now. Once in a while though, he worked up his courage and asked to read out loud. He'd raise his hand enthusiastically, practically lifting himself out of the chair. When I saw that, I made a point of calling on him immediately and made a special effort to praise him when he did a good job.

One day when the class was walking in a line on our way to lunch, James found it important to talk. (I always wondered why teachers walk kids in lines.

It seemed to be so ridiculously important to walk students in straight, quiet lines. Some teachers even had kids put their hands behind their backs. Wanting to be a good teacher, too (as if making my students walk in straight, quiet lines made me a good teacher), I made sure my kids walked in the quietest and straightest of lines. On this day, I got tired of listening to James talk, so I asked him to wait for me by the classroom door until I returned from escorting the rest of the class to the cafeteria.

I was expecting him to pout the way he usually did when reprimanded, but this time, for some reason, maybe because I was coming back, he seemed not to mind. Maybe he figured that he would be getting some one-on-one time with me and made it worth his while. James thrived for that kind of time.

After escorting the rest of the class to the lunch area, as expected, I walked back to the classroom. James was still standing by the door. When I walked up to him, I gave him a look that said, "You're not in too much trouble kid, so don't worry about it." Not saying anything to him, I put my key in the lock and opened the door. Then I put my arm gently around his head, in headlock fashion and playfully dragged him over to the closet so that I could get some money out of my wallet. Originally, I wondered why was I exposing my valuable hiding spot to this kid. I didn't know for sure what kind of kid James was yet; for all I knew he could also be a great thief. From now on, at just about any time, he could go into my closet, take out my wallet, and steal all the money he wanted. Knowing this, I took the risk anyway.

Once I had my money, I put my arm back around James' head again and walked him out of the room. We walked into the hallway, out of the building onto the playground area towards the lunch line. Once we were on the playground, we began to walk a little faster. I was feeling a little playful, so, like a dance partner, I swung James around to complete a couple of loops.

When we arrived at the lunch line, James picked up his lunch. I bought the same lunch that the kids were eating that day—chicken, cornbread, and fruit salad—and then walked to the outside eating area to join James. I found him eating quietly by himself. We didn't talk much, but I did make an effort to question him about his homelife. James explained that he wasn't living with his father and he hadn't seen him in quite some time.

"Did you ever meet your father?" I asked.

He nodded his head yes, then opened up a little and said, "He's in jail."

Because I was curious, I asked, "Why's he in jail?"

James looked away and wouldn't tell me why. I guess asking about why a person's father was in jail was really none of my business.

James wasn't wearing a coat that afternoon and it was cold out. Heck, I wasn't wearing a coat and I was cold! So after we quickly finished our lunch, I asked James if he wanted to go back to the room to get his coat out of the closet. He nodded his head in agreement. Grabbing him around the head with my arm again, we started walking back towards the room.

When we were just about to reach the building our classroom was housed in, Mrs. Ruiz came walking by with another teacher. James was shuffling along with his untied gym shoes like he always did. I didn't much care about that, but Mrs. Ruiz certainly did. She yelled out, "Pick up your feet!" I almost died. The only contact she had with James all day, or all week for that matter, and this is what she had to say? I kept walking with my arm wrapped around his head, without saying anything to either James or Mrs. Ruiz. James didn't say anything either, but he did pick up his feet—for the moment at least.

After we got our coats out of the closet, I decided that I didn't want our time together to end, so I walked James back out to the playground (without my arm around his head this time) and took him over to the chin-up bar that was attached to the handball wall. At the time, we were the only ones out on the playground. All the other kids were still finishing their lunches.

"So, do ya think you can do a pull-up?" I asked.

James shrugged his muscular shoulders and said, "I don't know."

"Well, there's only one way to find out," I said as I hoisted him up to the bar. With no choice left to him but to try, the tough little guy cranked out six perfect-form pull-ups! According to his age group, this amount was at the top of the President's Council on Physical Fitness and Sports' fitness test. James was a champ! I always knew he was strong, but I had no idea to what degree. No wonder why the other kids never messed with him.

By this time I was really getting into our little work out session, so I asked James, "Do you think you can do any push-ups?"

James didn't even know what a push-up was! After I demonstrated, strongman James cranked out twenty-seven perfect-form push-ups! When we were finished playing around a little more with the push-ups, I asked, "How about sit-ups, James? Do you think you can do any of those?"

As usual, he shrugged his shoulders and said, "I don't know."

"Well, come on over here then," I said. Laying him down on the playground bench directly under the chin-up bar, I manuevered his legs into the proper angle and made him cross his arms over his chest. James cranked out twenty-one! I was proud, and he was obviously very happy.

By the time James had finished his sit-ups, we were joined by dozens of other kids recently dismissed from the lunch area. Apparently, they had been watching us from afar and now wanted to join in on the fun. So, I spent the better part of the lunch recess period helping other kids practice their chin-ups, push-ups, and sit-ups.

James' little brother Jamal, who was one of the first to join us, cranked out the same number of chin-ups as James. He even did them in better form than James. I was grinning from ear to ear. Many of the kids wanted to get in on the action.

As I sat there on the bench, watching the rest of the kids and James continue to test themselves on the various exercises, I realized that this was going to be the kind of teaching experience I would never forget. It was times like these that made me glad that I was a teacher. It was also the kind of experience that made me glad that I wasn't a principal rushing around the schoolyard with all kinds of ridiculous administrative concerns to take care of, only having time to yell at kids that were passing by to pick up their feet.

Keep a Look Out for Drugs, Guns, Knives, and . . .

A memo came from the office at the end of a particularly difficult day, just as the kids were getting ready to go home. The memo contained a school announcement that was due to go home with the kids. When I looked over the letter, I had a hard time believing what I read.

A form of tattoo called "Blue Star" was being sold to children. The tattoo, which was soaked in LSD, was actually a small piece of paper containing a blue star the size of a pencil eraser. Apparently, when the kids put the tattoo on, the drug was rapidly absorbed through the skin. In addition, brightly colored tabs, resembling postage stamps, with pictures of Superman, Mickey Mouse, Bart Simpson, butterflies, clowns, and various Disney characters, were being sold to kids. These tabs were laced with "acid." Any kid who bought and used the stamps would exhibit symptoms such as hallucinations, severe vomiting, uncontrolled laughter, mood changes, and changes in body temperature.

Needless to say, I was shocked. I couldn't believe it—drugs specifically designed to appeal to children! After distributing the memos to the kids, we read it over. When I asked my kids about the drugs, most of them already knew about the tattoos and colored tabs. Worse than that, some of my kids had already purchased the stuff! And a few of them could even tell stories about people they knew that had already used them and got sick from them!

When I stood at the front of the room, with my eyes bugging out and my jaw hanging down to my knees, my students were amused. I didn't mean for the look on my face to be amusing. I was shocked. Taking it all in stride, they got up out of their seats, got their bookbags and coats from the closet, and lined up quietly at the door. As they stood there waiting to be dismissed, they all looked at me as if I were a real greenhorn or something. James even shook his head and let out a contemptuous snort. Angela said, "Don't worry Mr. Gust, we won't mess with 'em." Having worked in the inner city before, I thought I had seen it all, but to them, true veterans of the 'hood, I was a little baby still wet behind the ears.

The next morning after signing in and picking up my things from my mailbox in the office, I made my way down the hall to my classroom. It was very early yet, so I walked down the silent hall alone. How calm and peaceful it was at that time in the morning when all the kids were probably still at home just now getting out of bed.

As I made my way out of the main building, I noticed that on the doors that opened to the building where my classroom was housed were three large posters. When I got close enough to read what they said, I stopped cold:

> See a Gun at School?
> Save a Life—Tell Someone
> HOTLINE 1-800-954-HELP
>
> See a Knife at School?
> Save a Life—Tell Someone
> HOTLINE 1-800-954-HELP
>
> See a Weapon at School?
> Save a Life—Tell Someone
> HOTLINE 1-800-954-HELP

What horrible posters to see at school! I hated seeing them there. I thought schools were supposed to be sanctuaries, places of peace and innocence. Back when I was at school in second and third grade, that's how they seemed to me. Things were changing, I guess. Schools were quickly becoming battlegrounds, just like everywhere else in the world. So much for our school creating a civil citizenry. Now we were supposed to look out for drugs, guns, knives, weapons, and who knew what else.

Later that day, after the kids had gone home, I decided to find out more about guns and weapons found on school grounds. I called the LAUSD Public Information Unit, Office of Communications, and spoke with a Public Information Officer. I told him that I was looking for information about guns and weapons recovered in the LAUSD. I told him about an article that appeared in the *Los Angeles Times*, which stated that in the 1991–1992 school year, 1,403 weapons were confiscated at the LAUSD's 650 schools. Thirty-three of those weapons were guns taken away from elementary students. The PIO didn't know about the article, but he did have information given to him by the School Police Department. It was a comparison of all weapons recovered by weapon type for the fiscal years 1992–1993 versus 1993–1994. According to the statistics, there was an eighteen percent drop in the amount of weapons recovered from year to year. The drop was attributed to the new discipline policy concerning weapons found on students. Seems as though immediate expulsion and metal detectors were helping to keep weapons at home.

That's what things had come to. Kids going to school, with concealed weapons, passing through metal detectors, getting expelled. Used to be, we'd watch for kids bringing apples to school. Who knows what we'd be watching for next?

The Shootings

The first I heard about the shooting was from one of the teacher's assistants at our school when she stuck her head in the door and motioned for me to come out in the hallway. After I followed her, it became obvious that she was shook up about something. Whispering softly, she explained that a little girl had just been killed in a drive-by shooting, near the school, several minutes prior.

Ms. Kelleher, the second-grade teacher from across the hall, was leaning in her doorway with her arms crossed, wearing her perpetual smile. Apparently she already knew about the drive-by. "I first heard about it when I was in the library with my class," she confessed matter of factly. Surprisingly, it didn't seem to bother her at all.

Knowing that nothing else other than a lot of empty talk would result of my being out in the hallway, without saying a word, I walked back into my classroom. As soon as I did, our principal's voice came over the intercom system. "Boys and girls, someone got hurt. But no one at school was hurt and you have nothing to worry about."

Hurt? Hell, someone was killed! And the kids didn't have to be told honestly by our principal, Mrs. Ruiz, to know. Some of them heard the teacher's assistant telling me. She really didn't whisper softly enough. Feeling it was time to be honest with all of them, I tried to help explain. "What you're going to find out when you go home is that someone was killed in a gang shooting."

Their response—no big deal! They barely looked up from their work. Instead of asking questions about the incident, they just continued gluing cotton balls onto their black construction paper to form our cirrus, cumulus, and stratus clouds. We were working on the children's book *Bringing the Rain to Kapiti Plain,* so for a science lesson, we were learning all there was to know about the rain cycle and clouds in the sky—especially the stratus variety, since they were the rain clouds illustrated in the story.

Several minutes later, while the class was still busy working, we heard several sirens scream by the school. Our room was right off 104th street, so we could hear the noise quite clearly. I looked up from what I was doing to watch how the kids would react and noticed that they barely noticed at all. They just kept right on working. Either they really liked working on their science–art project, or the sirens and commotion meant nothing to them at all.

Later, after everyone had gone home, I found out from Anthony, one of the campus aids who lived nearby, that there was a little fight going on between the gangsters in the Hacienda Village and Nickerson Gardens housing developments. According to Anthony, they were arguing about who could sell what drugs where. The gangsters from "Nicks," as they were called, wanted more room to sell their drugs. They wanted to sell in Hacienda Village, too. Apparently, when one of the negotiating gangsters pulled out his gun, the opposing gangster said that he would go home and get his gun, too, if that was the way he wanted to play it. Soon after, the shooting started. Turns out that three people were shot. The first two were gangsters, and they were only injured. The third was a little girl who was standing nearby. She was killed.

At the time, what amazed me most was how the children, and local residents, accepted the crime and violence. It was commonplace, almost as though nothing much really happened. People, and the kids, just went about their business as usual. I, on the other hand, like the teacher's assistant who delivered the news, was all shook up.

The day after, when I returned to school, I discovered that some of what had happened was in fact untrue. Funny, how rumors start through thoughtless reactions. Yes, there was some shooting going on for the reasons that were explained, but nobody was killed. Thank God for that. However, two children were hurt. The first was a kindergarten student at our school. She was shot in the head. Fortunately, the bullet only grazed her skull, but a fragment of the bullet was still lodged in her brain. She was doing rather fine at Martin Luther King Hospital. Word had it that she was sitting up in bed, laughing, and talking about school. Her mother was considering leaving the lodged bullet fragment in her brain. The other young child was a Latino boy, not yet in school. He was shot in the arm.

We discussed all of what I discovered in class that day. I apologized to my students for contributing to the spreading of the rumor, and of course they were all very forgiving. (I love little kids for that. They have to be the most forgiving people on the planet. I wish adults could be as compassionate and forgiving.) We talked about the neighborhood, about the safe and unsafe areas of the community. We talked about what we could do to maintain our own safety as well. I asked if anyone had ever seen a drive-by Many had. Some even told stories about being unfortunate victims of the constant onslaught of violence.

Donnell showed the class his gunshot wound from a prior incident. Several years ago, he had been shot in the knee. The scar from the bullet wound was still visible. When it happened, he was shopping with his mother at the Dr. Martin Luther King Jr. Shopping Center right around the corner from our school. He and his mother came out of a store at the same time that a bunch of gangsters were driving by in a car. When they started shooting, Donnell was hit. The bullet grazed one knee and lodged into the other. He spent two days in the hospital.

James, too, had a story to tell. He showed the class the gunshot wound on his back. He, too, had been grazed by a bullet. For some reason, though, I had a hard time believing him. It seemed that he was just trying to match Donnell's story somehow. Maybe I just didn't want to believe that all these kids had either witnessed, or been a victim of, drive-by shootings. Maybe James was romanticizing the idea of the tough life in the inner city. But then again, maybe I was wrong; the other kids seemed to believe his story.

Later that day, after all the stories were told, after all the mess of rumors were cleared up, when all the kids were out in the hallway all lined up to go home, James' mother appeared at school. Turns out that James' younger brother Jamal had gotten himself into some serious trouble. Jamal was in first grade, and had quite a notorious reputation for being a holy terror.

I could've guessed what it was all about, because earlier in the day, when I picked up the class from the playground after lunch, I watched James try to explain to his brother that he had to protect and stick up for himself. Apparently Jamal listened to his brother's advice, because when I saw their mother, standing in the doorway of the room next door with her slippers on, she was carrying not one, but two big whipping sticks. These weren't any small twelve-inch rulers or anything like that, but rather two long, skinny tree branches that she had apparently stripped from a local tree, probably while making her way to school.

She didn't say much to Ms. Mecca (Jamal's teacher) or her two sons. She just looked at Jamal and James with a stern face. And as all the children started walking down the hallway, the wrathful mother also walked, in silence, carrying her two big whipping sticks.

It was obvious that she had absolutely no shame about the whole affair. She carried an air about her that said, "This is the way it is. This is what I'm going to do to my kids, and if you don't like it, too bad." It also said, in some strange way that I'm not sure I'll ever understand, "Love." I don't know how getting a whipping could be an expression of love, but it sure seemed like it at the time.

As the two boys followed their mother down the hallway, James and Jamal, who were dressed exactly alike, kept right on talking to one another. I tagged along, attempting to listen to what they were saying. From what I could make out, it sounded like James was still trying to give his brother some advice. "That's why you're gonna get a whippin', Jamal," James said.

The two boys took the whole incident in stride. Neither one of them seemed scared. If the kids were going to survive in this neighborhood with all of its shootings and violence, they were going to have to be tough, I guess.

When Will It All Stop?

The following day, while my students were out on the playground for Physical Education, all the second- and third-grade teachers were having a meeting in Ms. Kelleher's room. We were trying to decide how much time to designate for specific areas and topics of future staff development. After making our decisions and concluding the meeting, the other teachers and I exited Ms. Kelleher's room to return to our classrooms. While in the hallway, we all noticed Jobay's mother and older brother walking down the hall. Jobay had been absent from school for a couple of days. With things being as busy as they were, I neglected to call Jobay's home to talk with his mother to find out why.

The mother and her son walked down the hall with an obvious downtrodden look on their faces. They seemed to be saddened by something. When Jobay's mother walked up to the group of us teachers, she proceeded to explain, in Spanish, that Jobay's oldest brother had accidentally killed himself while fooling with his gun in his bedroom. Her oldest son was sixteen.

Continuing to explain, tears began to slowly pour out of Jobay's mother's eyes. In turn, this made tears stream out of her younger son's eyes as well. As the other teachers continued asking questions, in Spanish, I tried my best to understand. You see, Yo hablo muy pequito Espanol (I speak very little Spanish.) And the Spanish that I do know comes in the form of commands: *Sientate*! (Sit down); *No mas hablan*! (No more talking!); *Caminar*! (Walk!); *Escribe el nombre en la papel*! (Write your name on your paper!); *Escuchen*! (Listen!); and so on. I was pretty pragmatic about my Spanish, and I noticed that these words quickly became my "essentials" when working with Spanish students. Pretty sad, huh? I never bothered to learn the Spanish language. It's not that I didn't want to be able to communicate with Spanish-speaking people, it's just that I never took the time, or extended the effort, to learn the language. My mind always seemed to be so preoccupied with too many other things.

Standing there in the hallway, I tried to understand the essence of what was being said. The teachers tried to accommodate my lack of understanding by translating now and then, but they were too engaged in the conversation to slow down for my benefit. However, I did get to ask some penetrating questions about the incident and discover some facts

After Jobay's mother finished explaining all the details, she and her son came to my room to get homework for Jobay. She wanted to find things that would keep Jobay's mind off of his brother. Apparently, Jobay was taking his brother's death pretty hard. After giving them all the work (reproducible worksheets) I thought Jobay could handle, they thanked me and made their way to the door. When they reached the door, Jobay's brother saw the picture of the class that I had posted on the bulletin board. The picture was taken in our school's auditorium during an assembly that we had a few weeks earlier. In the photo, Jobay was standing next to me. I had my arm around his shoulders and his head was pressed up against my side. The mother smiled slightly, seeming to appreciate my protective gesture towards her youngest son.

When my students returned from Physical Education, I told them why Jobay had been absent. I was totally surprised when I found out that many of them already knew. Donnell explained to the class that the word out on the streets was that the whole affair wasn't an accident. He had heard that Jobay's oldest brother killed himself because he was in trouble with both the gangs *and* the police. Knowing Donnell and how much he got around, his story was probably the most accurate. When all the discussion had subsided, Angela suggested that we write letters to Jobay expressing our condolences. We started right away.

The following day, while we were busy completing our sympathy cards, I began to think that it might be a good idea to walk over to Jobay's house to give him our cards personally. I asked the class, "You know, I've been thinking. How many of you think it would be a good idea to walk over to Jobay's house today after school to give him our cards personally?"

"That's a great idea, Mr. Gust," voiced Angela

"OK, then, how many of you would like to go along?"

Several of them raised their hands. Daniel said, "Mr. Gust, I can take you to Jobay's house. I know where he lives. He lives right next door to me."

"That'll be great Daniel."

So it was decided. We would finish our cards that day and then walk over to Jobay's house to give them to him right after school.

At the end of the day, while standing in the doorway to watch all my kids line up to go home, I asked Daniel, "How long do you think it will take us to walk to Jobay's house?"

"Four and a half minutes," announced the little soldier. Daniel must have timed his walk home for his parents. They probably wanted to know how long it took for their son to get home safely. My guess was that if Daniel took longer than four and a half minutes, they probably sent out a rescue squad.

Noticing that Ms. Kelleher was also standing in her doorway lining up her students, I asked, "Ms. Kelleher, a group of us are going to walk over to Jobay's house to give him our sympathy cards. Would you and any of your students like to join us?" She had Jobay's younger sister in her class, so I thought she and her students might also like to pay a visit. (Jobay had been held back one year, so he and his younger sister were in the same grade.) "Yeah, that sounds like a good idea. Hold on," said Ms. Kelleher, as she quickly darted back to her desk to grab her students' sympathy cards to bring along.

As Ms. Kelleher and I led our classrooms down the hallway, out of the building, only two other students besides Daniel said that they could go along. Lakima would come with me, and Ana, one of Ms. Kelleher's students, would walk along with her mother.

When we got to Jobay's house, four and a half minutes later, all three of the children were there. The first to greet us was Jobay's older brother. Jobay's mother wasn't at home, but the grandmother was. While Ms. Kelleher talked with the grandmother in Spanish about the details, I tried to make connections with the children in the room. I didn't do a very good job of it though; I didn't know what to say. Mostly, I looked at the faces of some of the girls and smiled. They were eating sandwiches at the time.

Jobay had been back in his bedroom when we arrived. When his older brother brought him out, it was obvious that he was the most affected by his oldest brother's death. The grandmother explained that Jobay used to sit in the window like a faithful little dog and wait for his oldest brother to come home. Jobay was wearing one of his brothers T-shirts, which the grandmother said he wouldn't take off.

Jobay took a seat on the couch, and I leaned over and gave him the cards that his classmates had made. Lakima reached over and gave Jobay the card that she made and uncomfortably said that she was sorry about his brother. I was amazed at Lakima's maturity and compassion. I would never have thought that she would choose to come along. As Lakima and I went through the cards with Jobay, showing him what people drew and what they wrote, he sat there lifelessly staring at the cards, barely able to respond.

When Ms. Kelleher got all the details about the wake from the grandmother, which was to be held the following day, we thanked everyone and left to return to school. Ana and her mother stayed.

As we reached the sidewalk in front of the house, a car pulled up in the driveway next door. I looked in the car and noticed one of my students from Figueroa Street School, where I had taught fourth grade several years ago. It was Martin! He was sitting in the passenger side of the car, looking cool. I said, "Hey Martin, how ya doing?"

"Hi Mr. Gust," Martin said back. His English was much better than I remembered it.

"You staying out of trouble, Martin?" Martin was always on the mischievous side when I knew him.

Martin grinned widely, "No."

Smiling back, I said, "Figures!" and kept walking.

When we reached Daniel's house, Lakima, Ms. Kelleher, and I said goodbye to him, waved, and continued walking through Hacienda Village back towards school. Just as we were nearing our school, one of Lakima's guardians (Lakima was living in a group home) aggressively walked up to us. Before even saying "Hello," she asked curtly, "Who are you!?"

I explained that I was Lakima's teacher and that we had just been to Jobay's house to give him our sympathy cards. She loudly explained how she had been waiting for Lakima, expecting to pick her up after school by the main entrance a half hour earlier. She looked worried and angry. Ms. Kelleher, sensing danger or an argument brewing, quickened her pace towards school, leaving me there to iron out all the difficulties. I did my diplomatic best by apologizing and taking responsibility for the situation. After she calmed down, I told her about the wake the next day and Lakima's request to go along. I told her that I promised Lakima that I would take her if she had permission. The guardian told us that Lakima would bring a note the next day if she had permission to go along. Lakima got in the car, and as the guardian sped away, I could hear her yelling at Lakima for causing her so much trouble.

The next day, Lakima did not bring a note giving her permission to go to the wake. To be quite honest, I was glad that she didn't. Glad because I didn't think I could bring myself to go. I have always hated wakes, and this time, I didn't think I would have the stomach to attend. All day long in school, I kept thinking of every one of the family members crying their hearts out and me standing there with my hands in my pockets not knowing what to do. I knew that my presence would or could provide some support to the family, and Jobay, but for some reason—call it a lack of character or responsibility—I couldn't get myself to go.

I was feeling overwhelmed by everything: James' father in jail; the memo warning kids and their parents about drugs; the posters about guns, knives, and weapons at school; the recent shooting in Hacienda Village; the constant onslaught of sirens and helicopters overhead; all my students' stories of drive-by shootings; and now this. Throughout the day, I found myself running my hands through my hair in an attempt to relieve some of the pressure, asking over and over, "When will it all stop?"

The only thing I wanted to do was to get in my car and drive to the beach as fast as I could so that I could have a beer, watch the sunset, and forget about this neighborhood, my students, and their difficult lives. And that's exactly what I did. Except the only thing I found myself doing while sitting in the bar, with my beer, looking out over the ocean, was contemplating what we were doing in our schools and how ineffective it all seemed to be. What we were giving our kids didn't seem to be enough, or didn't seem to be the right things. It had to change, but how?

Our Philosophical Framework? What's That?

Teachers need a plan to organize what they are attempting to build. An architect wouldn't build a house without a blueprint! An architect wouldn't take a pile of bricks and, willy-nilly, begin to build! An architect should be able to explain why he chose bricks over stucco, or wood over steel, just as a teacher should be able to explain why she employs one technique over another, or articulate how those techniques contribute to her overall goals for her students' growth and learning.

If we teachers were really interested in becoming professionals, it would certainly prove useful to have an understanding as to the philosophical foundation of our practices. When considering the statement, "My philosophy is . . ." we'd have to stand back from the ephemeral urgencies of teaching and living to form a comprehensive overview that would embrace both value–commitments and beliefs about the general nature of our actions. Sadly, it's rare that we teachers take the time to step back from our work to ask why we do what we do. We don't often know what assumptions we have in regard to our actions, beliefs, and values.

I certainly didn't. I didn't really know what my philosophy of teaching was. I was never given much of an opportunity to think it through. Never given a chance to ask myself the really tough questions about education. In most of my education as a teacher I was always given practical techniques. Such was the case with all the inservices and trainings I attended. I'd often hear or read the statement: "Receive ready-to-use materials and techniques that you can use in your classroom tomorrow!" Every once in awhile, I'd ask a question about educational theory or philosophy, and most of the teachers present would look at me as if I were a total nuisance. It always seemed that people all around me kept saying, "Never mind the reasons why we're doing something, just give us something we can use. We need it for tomorrow! We've got to have it now! We've got kids in our classroom and we've got to keep them busy; we have got to teach them something!"

I never understood this. It seemed to me that if we took the time to really look at our practices and situations, we would be more capable of seeing the systemic structures or patterns of behaviors that encompass the typically reactive pendulum swinging of education. We'd have a chance to become aware of the "Grandfather Clock" to which the constantly swinging pendulum of techniques is attached.

So here we all were, all us teacher-technicians at our school, attending a special staff development session on a Saturday. On this particular Saturday, Mrs. Ruiz was leading the small percentage of our school's teachers that was present through a staff development. Small percentage, because nobody wanted to be at school on a Saturday. Not that I blamed them, of course; I wondered myself why I didn't stay in bed and relax like the rest of the staff that stayed home that morning.

Anyway, during this staff development, Mrs. Ruiz started off with a review of our program's belief or mission statement. We discussed the many different aspects of our so-called beliefs or mission, which in some ways was really a defining of our philosophical framework.

We talked at length about what I call "Learning a New Language." It was the economically driven purpose of our Eurocentric society to teach the predominantly Hispanic, Black, Asian, and other non-Anglo children that speak Spanish, African American Language, Black English, Ebonics, or whichever language the children were speaking in our schools, something we were now calling Mainstream American English, or MAE.

Sadly most teachers referred to it as "Cash English." In other words, we were supposed to teach the children the "King's English" (another commonly used phrase) because with it, they would reap the same monetary, green and golden rewards as the King of England; the almighty dollar—the force that drove us. Our job was to teach the essentials—those things that each child would need to know to get a good job. Give the kids those short-term survival skills that are needed to make it in the world today.

Sitting there listening, I began to realize how tired I was of teaching children just the essentials. I was tired of teaching kids how to simply make it, or get over, or fit in. Oh, I understood the "making it" mentality all right, but I was growing tired of teaching children how to cope with the everyday pains of living. As far as I was concerned, especially after witnessing so many of our problems recently, we had too many pains to cope with. And the ways of coping weren't too effective either. Our living pains needed to be addressed, of course, but now I was feeling that the only way to address the pain was to try to change the world, instead of our minds. I personally wanted to go beyond the essentials.

I wondered, is that all there is to life? Is life nothing more than personal survival in a meaningless and unfriendly world? Now that I had an opportunity to see the conditions of our social "dis"-order in Watts, I was beginning to think that education and schools had better fast become an agent that would work to somehow transform the social order.

Unfortunately, however, due to the concensual thinking of our time, the primary reason I was there was to help my students eventually get a job! Was that all education was for, I wondered? Just to help the populace get a job? Is school just for enabling children to compete and win in the global economy? Were our children becoming just another product or resource that our country's labor force could exploit? Were schools just another industry looking to produce compliant and reliable workers? Whatever happened to children being the central concern of education, rather than business opportunity and economics? I don't know; maybe I stood alone in this, but I had always thought that education was much more than all that. I always thought of education as . . . well, learning, growing. You know, the relentless pursuit of thoughts and ideas, the finding of ourselves, the asking and attempted answering of questions such as Who am I? Where did I come from? Where am I going? What am I here for? How do we really want the world to be? What will we have to do to help make it that way?

Did education have to be so trite and mundane? Did the objectives of education have to be based solely on the perceived needs of society in general? What about the expressed needs of the children? Did we just want to produce mindless, unquestioning citizens that were incapable of thinking critically about what was happening in the world? Did we just want to produce citizens that could keep the economic system in our world running faster and faster? Was our sole purpose just to consume? My God, the industrialists, the business world, really had us running. The essentials, that's what we needed! Teach the essentials so that our children can get a job!

But what if there were no jobs once the child left school? What would happen then? What would our children do with the essentials then? I know; they could go ask the guys hanging out all day long in the parking lot on the south side of the Hacienda Village housing development next to our school. They'd tell the kids what to do. They'd tell them how they could use their acquired essential skills to get by. The kids could watch them use their essentially acquired math skills as they count the wads of money that they earned from selling drugs. They could tell the kids how they used the essentials to read all the forms they were required to fill out to apply for public housing or how to get on welfare. Oh yeah, the essentials alone were doing us a whole lot of good.

So, after we finished our "Learning a New Language" discussion, we progressed or regressed, I'm not sure which, into the topic of making sure that within our classroom instructional program, we aligned, in complementary fashion, our philosophical framework, instructional strategies and curricular testing. As I saw it, this is where we, as a staff, ran into another problem.

First of all, none of us really knew what our personal philosophy of education was. Furthermore, I doubted that any one of us really remembered the many philosophies introduced to us in our Foundations of Education class. And it's doubtful that the California Commission on Teacher Credentialing ever gave the laborious task of developing a philosophy of education its proper emphasis in teacher education anyway. Moreover, due to the way the district was awarding emergency credentials to college graduates from fields other than education, it's doubtful that many of the new teachers present in our school ever *had* a class that introduced them to the many philosophical orientations of education. As a result, nobody really knew what their philosophical orientation towards education was. And because most of the teachers present probably didn't want to put in the time and effort required to discover what their philosophy of education was, we uncritically followed the dominant, consensual philosophical orientation that our school system blindly supplied. Critical thinking in the schools?! Sheep, that's what we were! All of us, in our herd, passively consuming the nondiscretionary values and beliefs of the established institutions. Sheep, baa, baa, baaing all the way to the sheering pit.

But what if teachers were to become tenacious and independent enough to eventually determine their philosophical orientations? And what if their philosophical orientations did not coincide with the one that our school or district supposedly adhered to? Would the problem get even worse? Or would the conflict subside because teachers, in order to keep their jobs, subjugate or compromise their beliefs in order to swim the mainstream? Like everyone else trying to cope, teachers did need to make a buck, put food on the table, and pay the bills. What would happen?

I was growing very tired of our meeting that Saturday afternoon. It felt like I was the only one in the room actually questioning what we were doing. And it was becoming evident that most of the teachers were getting very tired of putting up with me. Nobody really wanted to think that Saturday morning. Nobody really wanted to put up with all my probing, questioning, wondering. Nobody really wanted to put in the effort to take a step back from our teaching practices to get a broader view of things so that we could really discover and define our philosophy of education. Everybody wanted to accept things as they were. I got the impression that my colleagues wanted to show up, put in their time, and collect their pay—good, essential, put-the-money-in-the-pocketbook skills. I certainly wasn't making any friends with my constant questioning. I was just prolonging our meeting and making it more difficult than it needed to be.

Really, all that I was doing was getting us nowhere fast. During a break, one teacher actually came over to me and whispered, "John, you think too much." Realizing then that there was nothing I could do to change things, I conceded and finally shut up. I put all my concerns aside and kept my mouth closed. I put my time in just like everybody else, signed my name on the sign-in sheet for the day to prove that my body was present, and waited for the very slight increase on my next paycheck for having been there that Saturday.

During my drive home from the meeting, I attempted to recall how we teachers typically determined our philosophical framework, position, or orientation in regard to how it guides the purposes, methodologies, and day-to-day concerns of teaching. I thought back to my relatively short formal training and remembered that, traditionally, the particular philosophies were explained to us student-teachers in our Foundations of Education class. Once we student-teachers became acquainted with the particular philosophies and educational theories, we were then invited to choose the one that we felt we "fit in."

There were myriad problems inherent in this approach. Foremost, it was next to impossible to adequately learn all the particular philosophies of education in the brief time period that a single one-credit-hour college class offered! From my recollection, the class covered philosophies and theories of education in a total of one chapter in our textbook, and at most, in two one-hour classes. And if I remembered correctly, we also had several other objectives covering various social, cultural, historical, political, and teaching as a profession issues to address. Moreover, we were never really given an opportunity to experience the day-to-day practices of these various philosophies. Merely studying each philosophy was nothing more than an intellectual exercise—one could know a philosophical stance only conceptually unless it is fully experienced. Therefore, I reasoned that it was ridiculous to assume that this approach would ever allow any student-teacher to become capable of truly determining a good and comfortable "fit."

So rather than going directly home, knowing that the local libraries would be closed, I drove to the nearest Border's bookstore. After arriving, rather than heading towards the education section, I walked straight to the philosophy section. The way I figured it, it wasn't going to be possible to determine my philosophy of education, without also giving consideration to my philosophy towards life or worldview. Traditional philosophies refer to complete bodies of thought that present a world view of which education is part. Ultimately, then, it was necessary to slow down and step all the way back, in order to adequately determine how I inherently and naturally viewed the world first, before attempting to define my educational philosophy. It seemed to me, then, that that was basically what the process of determining one's philosophy of education was—a defining of one's "reality," or more accurately . . . a defining of one's self.

Making myself comfortable on the floor in front of the shelves, I pulled down as many books as I could find addressing the task at hand. In my brief survey of the disparate Western philosophies or worldviews, I was able to count out over forty—and who knows what philosophies I may have missed altogether. It is no wonder why educators rarely discover or define their philosophical orientations! And no wonder why we can't seem to properly align our educational philosophy with our teaching practices and assessments!

While studying all of the books on the floor in front of me, trying to ascertain the various philosophies or worldviews available to choose from, it soon became apparent that I was working backwards. There was no way I could ever hope to adequately understand all of the disparate philosophies in the short amount of time I had to work with. People have spent their whole careers attempting to do just that. The whole method of laying out the particular philosophical orientations or frameworks first and then deciding which one I fit into had to be wrong. It was like putting a bunch of "holes" in front of a "teacher peg" and asking that peg, who wasn't really sure what shape he was, to determine which hole he felt most comfortable fitting in. Imagine how many differently shaped holes he'd have to jump in and out of! Any good teacher knows that if you are going to teach something, then you have to start at the beginning. In this case, the beginning would be the individual.

That's a pretty profound task when you think of it. To my understanding, it was certainly not something that our schools spent time helping learners do! Schools leave learners on their own to accomplish that task. And sadly enough, more often than not, we never get around to doing it at all! Instead of fully differentiating ourselves both intrapsychically and interpersonally, in order to form a complete and stable self, we find some way of reshaping our "pegged selves" so that we can quickly fit into and fuse with whatever established "holes" are available. After all, most of us desperately long to fit in somewhere, don't we?

If, however, a teacher were fortunate enough to have stepped back from the transitory urgencies of life to fully differentiate in order to develop a clear understanding of who they are, how they view the world and reality, or what shaped peg they are, then, and only then, would they adequately know their basic beliefs about what schools are for, what schools should do, what is to be learned in school, how students learn, and who or what is given priority in schools. Only then would teachers understand which particular philosophical framework or orientation most aligns itself, or fits well with . . . the individual.

So there it was. My new direction was to spend my nonworking hours trying to define exactly who I was, how I viewed the world and reality, and finally what philosophy of education I held. For the time being, all I had was the hope that someday I might be able to understand reality in all its wonder. All I had was the desire to understand myself and find my true fit in the world, and in education. I just wished there were others willing to spend the time and effort to fully differentiate themselves to discover their own worldview or, more specifically, who they truly are.

The Proselyte

After that Saturday meeting, it became obvious that I was very confused. Having no real, firm idea what my own personal philosophy or worldview was, I decided to quit looking to others for answers and began the onerous process of looking within. Questioning everything, I began to wonder if what my colleagues and I were doing in schools was the right thing. In spite of all the pressures to conform to preestablished standards, I decided to follow my heart. It was time to change what I was doing in the classroom.

When I had first returned to teaching in the public school system, I knew that I would be required to teach in a way that was incongruent with my own ideals. And on top of that, I really didn't know what my ideals were, I just knew that what I was agreeing to do was significantly different from what I felt was the right thing to do.

After I had been hired on, I was also required to sign a form which generally stated that I agreed to teach the basics or essentials to my students. These basics or essentials would, of course, enable my students to score well on the competence-based test that the district provided. In essence, then, my teaching was due to be centered around the test. It quickly became obvious that I disliked that focus. I disliked it, but because, at the time, I needed the job more than I needed to follow my heart, I signed on. I was out of money; what else could I do?

However, as my lower level needs were eventually met, I began listening more and more to my heart . . . and common sense. What we were doing in our classrooms was dramatically missing the mark. It has been said that the essential task of public education is to civilize human beings, to make productive citizens of the populace, to create an industrious class of men and women who will obey the law, be diligent in their work, and add to the economic well-being of our country. But from all that I had encountered in Watts thus far, the methods that the school system employed to reach these goals weren't very successful. As far as I was concerned, we were in a state of profound social and cultural crisis. And the only thing that we were doing in education was to continue transmitting the social ills, symptoms, pervasive problems, and afflictions that were plaguing humankind.

The more thought I gave as to the purpose of education, the more I began to believe that schools should be a type of wall-less community center that worked to liberate and empower children. The only legitimate goal of a truly humane education, therefore, would then be to help my students learn that they were in control of their own destinies. And through this individual empowerment, the school would actually become an agent for social change.

And if I viewed school in this way, then maybe it was high time that I actually got involved in the task of awakening students' consciousness to the social problems surrounding them, not as a purely intellectual exercise, but in a way that would enable my student-learners to become actively engaged in the solving of problems in order to create a more egalitarian and cooperative society. I was becoming convinced that positive, constructive social change would arise if I began challenging obsolete conceptions of education, schooling, and instruction and engaged my students in dialogue that would foster the implementation of carefully planned and directed social action programs and projects—projects that would effect some change in the life of the surrounding community.

And if I truly believed in all this, and was willing to proceed in this new direction, I would have to be willing to engage my students in dialogue that would critically examine our cultural heritage and not be afraid to examine the most controversial of social issues. I also needed to look beyond the confines of the community that I was teaching within. In essence, I needed to become a proponent of an education that emphasized the international dimension of life, because in an interdependent world, the quality of human life needed to be considered and enhanced on a global basis. And lastly, if I were going to be on the cutting edge of change, I knew that I would have to be prepared to be in the center of a storm of controversy.

As I gave thought to all of this during the remainder of the weekend, it became more and more evident that I was through with using the curriculum to transmit subject content into the minds of students. Instead, the curriculum had to emanate from the child rather than from state boards of education. As much as possible, my students needed to be free to develop naturally, and to do so, I would have to focus more on them rather than on any predetermined curriculum.

Certainly, I was tired of relying exclusively on bookish methods of instruction—textbooks and scripted, teacher-proof curriculum guides. And I surely didn't feel it was appropriate for my students to learn passively by simply memorizing factual data. Instead, I wanted to emphasize activities and experiences. I wanted to encourage cooperative group learning activities rather than competitive individualized lesson learning. In practice, I wanted to actually become more of a resource person, facilitator, and guide to learning.

I also condemned my role as an authoritarian teacher. I was appalled by the use of fear or punishment as a form of discipline. If I had my way, I would find some method, even with my young students, to form a democratic classroom environment. And I would use these democratic procedures as a prelude to any social action project that would promote community reform. That meant that I would also have to disregard the all-too-common four-walls philosophy of education that isolated my work from the social realities surrounding my classroom.

And lastly, and perhaps most importantly, I wanted what I did in my classroom to become a laboratory for educational experimentation and impetus for pedagogical reform. In other words, I wanted to become an explorer of sorts. An explorer that engaged in unofficial action research projects that could eventually be used to inform and educate the public in a broader context.

So, before returning to work on Monday, I said to myself, "I'm going to do things my way for once, and I'm not going to worry about the consequences." I changed my reasoning, my thoughts, my way of doing things. When I returned that early Monday morning, I put away all the reproducible basic-skill worksheets and scripted, programmed, mindless, robotic curricular guides that I had been using. I stopped worrying about the test; in fact, I wasn't test-driven at all. Rather, I vowed that I would be child-driven. In some way, I wanted to facilitate the active transformation of my students and the immediate environment.

The first thing that I decided to do was to create a democratic learning environment. Unfortunately, I had no idea how to do it! To guide me, I only had a very simple introduction of the progressive ideas of John Dewey. Certainly, I had no clue as to how I would apply those thoughts on democracy and education. And from my teacher education days, when I took the Foundations of Education class, I wrote a term paper on the Swiss educator Johann Heinrich Pestalozzi. Remembering his general methods, which called for educators to be loving persons who attempted to create a homelike school environment, I set off in my new direction.

Who's the Boss?

My challenge, as I saw it, was to find a way for my students to actually teach me. I wanted them to teach me what and how they most wanted to learn. If I were going to do that, I would need to follow my students for a change—if that were possible. And if I were going to follow my students, I had to find a way to get them to feel, to know, to understand that we were equal—that we, student and teacher, were standing on the same ground.

First thing Monday morning, I told my kids straight out, "From now on we're going to change the way we do things in class. We're not going to be using these ditto sheets, with the fill-in-the-blank questions, anymore. We might not even have spelling words every week, unless you want them. That means no more "Say the word, spell the word, say the word" drills. We might not line up, or try to line up, in straight, silent lines anymore. But you know what we're going to do? We're going to find a way for you to tell me what we're learning for, what you want to learn, and how you want to learn."

When I explained this, many of them looked at me with entirely blank faces. Jose's eyes, however, were practically bugging out of his head. You could tell his brain was up to something. He was excited about the idea. Some of the others were smiling, and probably thinking, "Oh-boy! Could we take advantage of this joker." I could only imagine what outrageous, devious things they might be thinking.

I wasn't sure if they completely understood that I was going to facilitate an equal teacher–student relationship, so I immediately thought of a way to explain it so that they would grasp the idea. I knew that the greater than (>) sign that we recently covered in math would explain the concept perfectly. I walked over to the chalkboard, picked up a piece of chalk, and drew four stick people on the board. After labeling them—administrator, principal, teacher, and student—I drew little greater than signs in between each.

Administrator > Principal > Teacher > Student

I continued to explain: "This is typically how things work in most schools. Most of the time, the teacher is 'greater than' the students, the principal is 'greater than' the teachers, and the administrators or school district's superintendents are 'greater than' the principal." They knew immediately what I meant. Light bulb on!

Looking out over their shining faces, I picked up an eraser from the ledge and said, "But we, in our classroom at least, are going to erase that big, nasty ol' 'greater than' sign between the teacher and students. And in its place we are going to put an equal sign." In a dramatic swoop of my arm, I erased the greater than sign and replaced it with an equals sign. They clearly understood this concept.

Administrator > Principal > Teacher = Student

Feeling rather proud of myself for explaining this advanced concept to their elementary minds, I stood there gloating for a moment. The first question came from Jose: "Does that mean that we can call you John?"

Lakima followed, "We don't have to call you Mr. Gust anymore?!"

I laughed. And then thought about Jose's question for a moment. What a treasure! To be called John again. A long time ago, in my first year of teaching, I didn't want to be called "Mr. Gust." But now, as a weathered, veteran teacher, I wondered what my colleagues would think and say. I imagined they would say something like, "Oh, brother, what a naive 'Don Quixote,' dreamer of a teacher you are." Then I thought, do I really care what my colleagues have to say? So I told the kids, "Yeah, you can call me John. But outside our classroom, I'm not so sure it's a great idea. Maybe you can call me John in the classroom, but outside the classroom, you should probably still call me Mr. Gust."

But then, with their bestowed authority to now call me John, something peculiar started to happen. A dissipation of control was immediately experienced. I was giving it up, and, due to human nature, this "control" was looking for somewhere else to go. Maybe it was Lakima, but then again it could have been Natasha, or Lashea, Danyell, Devon, or who knows. Fact is, I didn't hear who the question came from: "Then who's going to be the boss?"

The demon was exposed: control—an amazing, living, consuming drive desired by many, acquired by few. But why? Could it be because so few of us really had it? It's true. If more people were willing to give away some of the power and control that they worked so hard to attain, the world would certainly be a much less dysfunctional place. If some of the people living in Watts could be made to feel as though they had some of it—really had some of it—I believe there would be less violence, less destruction, less need to escape through drugs, and more real learning going on in the classroom. If people, children, could deeply feel and truly know that they had power and control, they could escape from their feelings of helplessness and become functional, participative, contributory and responsible citizens. If the subjugated and oppressed were really given a voice that was heard, acknowledged, validated, and put to use, I truly believe that they would respond in a way that actually helped to improve their condition. These kids didn't need to merely learn their "A,B,C's," or their "3 R's," or their standardized basic skills! Who gave a damn about their test scores anyway?! What they needed was power and control—and the responsibility that went with it.

At that moment, I was faced with a dilemma. Now that I was giving away some of my control and power, how was I going to keep some sense of order and structure in my classroom? In which direction would our learning go? Would there be any learning taking place at all!? Could it be that the very structure of the classroom system would need to dissipate and endure a state of unaesthetic chaos for a period of time before transcending into something more empowering? Would I be able to stand the inevitable noise and confusion? And how would I be able to stimulate those students that had always been so passive to speak up and be counted? Would they grab some of the power and control that was their due? Or would they continue to be run over by the overly aggressive ones? I had so few healthy, assertive students in my class.

I could probably count on Angela, Raynell, and Jennifer, with their advanced morality and assertiveness, to pull the classroom along. Eventually, James, Antoine, Jose, Danyell, Lakima, Lashea, and Natasha would let go of the aggressive behavior they occasionally exhibited. And Ashley, Leslie, Donnell, and Jasmine, with some encouragement, would eventually become less passive. As for Devon, Jobay, Roberto, Kevin, Jamie, and Tory, well, I was doubtful that they would ever figure it out. I hated to say it, but sometimes they seemed so lost. But who knew, Kevin might surprise us all. He was becoming more and more confident.

As for who was going to be boss, well, we'd just have to see. Hopefully, we *all* would . . . with an entirely new definition of the term.

Democratic Dogs

We started pretty loose at first. I wanted the kids to get a sense of freedom, give them some running room, let the control or structure dissipate, before any constraints were placed on them. At first, I was loath to make suggestions as to what they should do. With no methodology available to help design our democratic environment, I basically surrounded them with as many objects and materials as I could get my hands on, and then left them entirely to themselves. Not wanting their freedom to be infringed upon, I was even apprehensive about suggesting what might be done with the materials.

Right away, I got a good chance to see who the aggressives, assertives, and passives were. The aggressives took off like wild dogs unchained. They ran around the room sniffing here, sniffing there, looking here, looking there, panting, leaving their "mark" in various places around the room, and generally destroying everything in their path. The passives, once taken off the leash, became scared and ran directly to their little doghouses in the corners. But as for the assertives, far too few in my opinion, well, they just kept walking alongside of me as if nothing had happened. Together, we continued walking on our path towards competency, literacy, and higher order thinking. Together, we watched the aggressives run around destroying everything. Together, we watched the passives hide in their doghouses.

After a couple of days into the process, I wanted to kill the lot of them. Standing there, watching, pulling my hair out, I asked myself, "Why did I do this?" I gave up control, trying to create a democratic environment in the classroom, and the little people, at least the aggressive ones, went completely nuts! They were all over the place. And there seemed to be no end to the chaos. I tried to loosen up, be a little more permissive, be a little more patient, waiting for all the craziness to come to an end, hoping for some spontaneous emergence of order or self-organization, but it didn't come. The chaos continued.

After a while, I became overwhelmed by my naysayer attitude and thinking. I even considered taking back my power or even standing over them and ruling with an iron fist. Didn't these kids have any concern for anyone else? Were they so self-centered, so egocentric, that they had no insight, no sensitivity as to what they were doing to those around them? What was it that made one child so gentle, so sensitive, so perceptive of others, so concerned with being nice, while another child was so unaware, so uncaring, so selfish, so rude? Was it their personality, or was it something they were expected, almost rewarded, for doing? If that were so, who could be rewarding them for that behavior? Who actually reinforced the aggressive behavior of these boys? Why couldn't these boys be sensitive enough, caring enough, compassionate enough, polite enough to work things out in a friendly, calm way? Was their behavior biologically and genetically programmed or merely a response to their environment? Or was I simply expecting to much conventional morality from my second and third graders?

I had no idea how much more difficult a social structure a democracy would be to attain, and maintain, than an autocracy. As the autocratic leader of the class, I could tell the children exactly what to do, when to do it, and how to do it. I didn't have to provide reasons why. I could be oppressive, coercive, demanding, strict, and unconcerned with their emotional growth all at the same time. I could use overly simplistic behavioral management techniques and pass out rewards and consequences like they were going out of style. I could have order! I could give specific lessons at specific times for specific reasons. I could pass out assignments totally of my own choosing whenever I wanted. I could have a quiet classroom!

And who would care anyway? That was the way it had always been done. The teacher was the boss. Heck, I used to do it all the time! Besides, with absolutely no training on how to design a democratic classroom, I was becoming more and more aware of my own inadequacies—I was a terrible facilitator of learning. If I went back to the old way of teaching, I wouldn't have to watch them react to the "new" democratic philosophy with unorganized, sporadic, and what I considered to be rude behavior. I wouldn't have to watch all this disorder. I wouldn't have to be patient, hoping that time was all that was needed before the children decided to learn and interact with each other in a positive way. Within an autocracy, the class would be calm and quiet, and would work diligently to improve their academic skills; they'd be reading from a quality literature selection, they'd be sitting in their seats, they'd be attentive, and they'd probably even be comfortable with all that I would be doing while back in control. I'd have my classroom, and the children in it, in the palm of my hand. I'd feel comfortable again.

Besides that, maybe trying to provide a fully and truly democratic environment was actually a detriment to a child's growth. Maybe the kids needed more than the course of a year to learn how to function in a democratic environment. Maybe learning to live in a democracy was something that took a long, long time. Maybe the kids would never truly be able to fully experience what it is like to live in a democracy anywhere or anytime, so why try to do it here, now in my classroom? I mean, really, which among the individuals living in poverty in Watts, ever actually felt as though they lived in a society that was fully democratic. It might be stereotypical or discriminatory thinking on my part, but the oppression and subjugation supported by bureaucratic, commmercial, and political superstructures had to be a huge part of their lives. It had to be; after all, it often felt that way for me! It had to permeate their lifes, so much so that their attitudes, perceptions, thoughts, beliefs, and behaviors probably perpetuated the very oppression that they were trying so desperately to overcome. And if our society were really willing to look at it closely and hard enough, I was sure that we would find the problem to be much more pervasive than most people were willing to admit. So what made me think I could do anything about it in one short school year? Why not give it up and go back to autocratic practices in my classroom? Nobody would care anyway.

Aside from not knowing how to facilitate a democratic classroom, I also began questioning whether I was a good enough leader. I knew that the crucial determinant of group atmosphere rested in its leadership, and the successful resolution of social conflict, inevitable in any context—let alone in a democracy—required the activity of a trained, orderly leader. Except I certainly wasn't properly trained by any means. This kind of leadership required much more than utilizing a few fancy tricks to make people "feel good." I could not simply be a clever persuader. The democratic process was complex, and it would be necessary for my students and me to play our respective roles within it. But what were those roles? Even we Americans, for all our familiarity with democracy, needed to continually practice and improve our group activities.

In addition to all that, I was also concerned that the pace of our learning would be considerably slower within this new democratic context. I wanted the kids to learn a lot; I just wasn't sure what they most needed to learn. Fortunately, what kept me going was my interest in the learning process. It was clear that when my students proceeded at their own pace, learning was slower, but it was also of much higher quality.

The more I thought about it then, the more convinced I became that if my students were to become responsible, empowered participants in our democratic society, they would need to experience firsthand the democratic process.

Democracy emphasizes dialogue, negotiation, bargaining, and, ultimately, voluntary citizen cooperation by rational individuals well disposed toward the common welfare. And even though I wasn't sure if my students were just yet rational or disposed toward our common welfare, I knew that if our democratic state were to be productive, they would need to learn how to talk with one another civily, how to negotiate agreements, how to bargain or compromise with others, and how to eventually become desirous of actively and courteously participating in our classroom community.

Democratic governments have always supported education for their citizens. Faith in the power of education is, after all, an integral characteristic of democracy. And rightly so. A democracy needs educated citizens who can think for themselves, citizens who feel responsible for taking part in public affairs, keeping informed on public issues, and voting intelligently. Therefore, our democratic institutions had to produce leaders worthy of public trust and responsibility. In my mind, the common practice of teaching rudimentary, basic academic skills wasn't enough. My students needed much more than the basics.

Another reason why I wanted to continue the democratic process was that if we look at common democratic ideals, it becomes apparent that widespread participation in politics does not necessarily ensure good government.

The effectiveness of a democratic government is dependent on the quality of participation. Well-informed and well-educated citizens might be able to participate more intelligently, but the best way to develop quality participants is to foster participation skills and democratic values in the classroom during a child's formative years, not after graduation.

And finally, the last motive for continuing my democratic teaching practices was that, deep down, I believed that all persons were equal in the sight of God. I believe that this dictum of faith plays a powerful role in shaping democratic political and social commitments in our country. The moral passion of democratic struggles historically has been derived from a prior set of commitments to principles of ontological equality in God's eyes. In our past, however, children have not been awarded the status of full personhood. I begged to differ with that position.

The world's largest minority, children, have forever been discriminated against, constantly considered too young to make their own decisions. But, in my view, my students had already reached full personhood. They might not have had all the experiences that I have had. They might not yet occupy all of the reasoning or moral capabilities that adults possess. And they probably still needed a great deal of guidance, care, and nurturance. But those human qualities of full personhood were inherent potentials already existing within the individuals in my classroom. And just because those inherent qualities were not fully expressed, there certainly was no reason for me to exclude my students from making decisions as to the policies that governed them. In our democratic society, there is no place for discrimination that prevents the emergence of respect and recognition for any group of people. Guiding children through the democratic process in the classroom would certainly be an appropriate way to foster the development of these inherent potentials. Therefore, my students would also enjoy the values of dignity and respect, and have a share in the power defining our classroom.

My decision to continue fostering a democratic classroom ultimately rested not only in my belief in the natural goodness of human beings, but also in my belief that all human beings are open to democratic responsiblity and possibility. I still had confidence that all my students would rise to these expectations. So, I put my concerns for the *process* of learning primary, and vowed to create a democratic learning environment.

Turning the Pack of Dogs into a School of Fish

Now that I was finally committed to creating a democratic classroom, it was time to get organized. It was time to get serious about organizing a democratic classroom. Trouble was, I still didn't know how.

Then, as I was scrounging through the literature books in the teacher's resource room one morning before school, looking for ideas, I found a book that I just *knew* would help. It was a story written by internationally acclaimed artist and sculptor Leo Lionni about a very smart and brave little fish named Swimmy.

Swimmy lived with his brothers and sisters in a happy but completely disorganized school of fish somewhere in a little corner of the sea—just like my classroom. Swimmy and all of his brothers and sisters swam around not as a team, but as a collection of individuals all heading in different directions at the very same time. They were all over the place, darting here and there, totally out of alignment, with all kinds of cross-purposes, in a complete state of chaos. Swimmy was a very fast swimmer, but unfortunately all of his brothers and sisters were rather slow. And, for some reason, Swimmy was black, while all of his brothers and sisters were red.

One day, as all the fish in the school were swimming around in their totally disorganized, unaligned way, a big, hungry fish darted by and gulped up all of Swimmy's brothers and sisters. But, because Swimmy was so fast, he was able to dive away. Now poor Swimmy was all alone, scared and sad in the deep, dark sea.

Fortunately, Swimmy didn't get too depressed. Instead, he kept busy continuing to swim along. As he was swimming, Swimmy encountered many new, marvelous creatures and quickly forgot all his troubles. He came upon a medusa, a lobster and some very weird fish that appeared to be pulled along by a thread. He also encountered some seaweed, an eel, and a few sea anemones.

Eventually, Swimmy met up with another totally disorganized, unaligned school of fish exactly like the one that had been extinguished. Swimmy quickly became friends with the new fish. He even tried to encourage his new friends to come out from their dark little corner so that they, too, could discover all the marvelous creatures of the sea, just as he had done. But his new friends argued with him, explaining that they didn't want to go because, if they did, the bigger fish would come along and devour them.

Tenacious little guy that he was, Swimmy didn't give up. Instead, he thought about the problem for a long time. And being the intelligent fish that he was, it didn't take too long for Swimmy to generate a marvelous idea! He wanted to design a totally new, organized school of fish that would serve to protect each other so that they could all go out into the sea together to explore all of its wonders. Swimmy explained to his new friends that he wanted to design a new, organized school, with the whole of them swimming together in unity so that they would resemble a great big fish. His new friends seemed to like the idea, so Swimmy taught them to swim in unity, with each fish having his or her own space. Eventually, the small red fish learned to swim together, in organized fashion, so that they actually did resemble a giant fish.

In the process, a commonality of direction emerged, they became harmonized and learned how to complement one another's efforts. They learned to swim in the groove, so to speak. Also, no one fish had to sacrifice its personal interests for the larger fish vision; rather, the shared vision actually became an extension of each fish's personal vision. There was less wasted effort, the chaos dissipated, and a type of resonance, synergy, and self-organization ensued.

Swimmy, the only black fish of the school, became the eye of the fish. He was the visionary, the principal designer, the one who helped guide the school. From then on, the new, organized school of fish swam together purposefully. They were free to venture out from their dark, oppressive corner and explore the wide-open, marvelous sea. In fact, they could actually chase the other big fish away!

As I finished reading the book, I knew that I had found exactly what I needed. I quickly grabbed the classroom set that was stored on the shelf, signed it out, and practically skipped back to the classroom. It was perfect! A disorganized school of fish? Swimmy, the principal design inquirer? I could use this book as a kick-off to get us organized. All kinds of cooperative, community-building activities could be brought in and connected to this book. Plus, if my students were willing, a wonderful thematic unit on the ocean or ecosystems could also be incorporated. We could learn how all of us, everywhere, are deeply interconnected in some unexplained way. The kids could learn all about medusas, lobsters, seaweed, eels, sea anemones, and whatever that weird fish that appeared to be pulled along by a thread was. I just hoped that we could swim as aligned as Swimmy and his new friends did.

The first thing we did that morning was to have a small conversation about what had been happening in the room. "You know what we've been trying to do in class, right?" They all nodded their heads. "What then, what is it that we've been trying to do? You tell me."

Jose, intelligent little fellow that he was, started first, "We've been trying to make our classroom a place where everyone is equal."

"Absolutely; that's totally correct," I responded.

"We've been trying to find ways for each of us to take responsibility for our own learning," Danyell added.

"Very good, Danyell," I said. She flashed that wide smile of hers.

"We've been trying to learn about things that we want, at our own speed, in our own way," explained the serious Raynell.

"Excellent. Now, has it all worked very well?" I asked.

A booming, "NO!" filled the room.

"I didn't think so either. That's why today we're going to begin doing things a little differently. Today, we're going to get organized. And I need your help."

I continued, "The first thing I thought we'd do was to read through this book that I have here. It's called *Swimmy,* and it's about a small little fish who lives somewhere in the corner of the sea. I think when we read through this book, you'll begin to notice that there are some similarities and differences between Swimmy and his brothers' and sisters' lives, and our lives here in our classroom. Let's read the book and see if you can point out the ways that Swimmy and his school of fish are very much like our classroom and very much different from the way things are as well."

I passed out the books. The first person to read was James, and when he had read enough, I asked him to pick the next person to read. We continued that way until we finished reading the entire book. I was proud and not too surprised that they were able to explain that we were just like Swimmy and his disorganized school of brothers and sisters. As expected, they were all capable of noticing how different Swimmy's new organized school of fish was from our situation in the classroom.

Just as we concluded our discussion of the similarities and differences, Kevin asked, "Mr. Gust, do you think we can get our classroom to swim together like one giant fish?"

I nearly fell out of my chair! But then I was totally shocked when Danyell added, "Yeah, I want us to be able to swim like a giant fish so that we can explore things just like Swimmy and his brothers and sisters did."

Jose put the icing on the cake when he said, "Mr. Gust, we're tired of messing around and going in all kinds of different directions." The pack of dogs was finally ready to become an organized school of fish.

"Alright then, yeah, sure, we can become an organized school of fish. But we'll need to decide upon a few things first. We need to talk about how we want to be in our classroom." So I explained about the three different ways that we could organize our pure, rather than representative, democracy. In language that they could understand, I explained participatory input, majority rule, and consensus building. After I was finished, they all just sat there looking at me, until Angela asked, "Can we use all three?"

Somewhat confused, I asked, "What do you mean?"

"Well," she continued, "sometimes you could get ideas from us and decide for the class. Other times, we could have a vote. And other times, we could talk things out until we all agree." What an intelligent kid Angela was! Why didn't I think of that? I guess, sometimes it takes a kid to figure things out.

Knowing we were on our way, I decided to keep the flow going. As long as they were all sitting in their seats, engaged in our conversation, I figured that I better start acting as Swimmy, by becoming the eye of the fish. They needed to learn how to swim together, with each person in their own place. "Okay, I think we need to set some general 'How to Swim' rules first. These should be rules for how we will discuss things."

"An important part of helping us to be an organized school of fish is to make the ground rules for participation. First I think each person should have a turn to speak, and each of us should be able to get equal time to talk. We should all speak only for ourselves, and speak with respect towards others. We should also keep ourselves away from trying to change others' opinions.

"Second, I think it will be important for each of us to listen to the person talking, with an open mind. Third, each person will take responsibility for talking only about the most important things. We shouldn't bring up something that has nothing to do with what we are talking about at the time. And last, and most importantly, we have to believe that each of us is a capable human being; that is, we all have to believe that we're all trying hard to do a good job."

"Does that sound agreeable to all of you?" I asked.

"Yeah, that sounds pretty good," said Raynell. The rest of the class nodded their heads.

"Good then. Now I need to ask all of you some questions so that I'll know exactly what you want. I think the first question should be, "How do you want our classroom to be?" I wrote the question on the board, circled it, and readied myself for clustering their responses. "Okay, so how exactly do you want our classroom to be? What kind of words can we use to describe how you would like our classroom to be? Somebody give me one word."

Kevin answered first, "Good!"

"Okay, that's a start. I'll write that down. Now what exactly do we mean when we say 'Good'; can anyone give Kevin some help?"

"Respectful," said Lashea.

"Helpful," said James. He always was a very helpful kid.

"Loving," said Jennifer. Wouldn't you know it.

"Sharing," said Natasha.

Then Devon added, "Quiet. We should be quiet when the teacher is talking." I wrote that down, wondering if Devon would ever actually be quiet himself.

"Nice," said Ashley. Nice could have been Ashley's middle name.

"Clean," added Jose. I liked that one. I was a neat freak too.

Then the answers seemed to flow. I couldn't tell where they were coming from: "stay together," "kind," "happy," "fun," "friendly," "sweet" (Jennifer had to offer that one), "smart," and, finally, "understanding."

"Excellent! You guys have done a great job. But now, before you go outside for recess, I want to ask just one more question. I need to know what you think makes a good teacher. In other words, what are the qualities of a good teacher?"

"What do you want to know that for?" asked Lakima.

"Well, I need to know because I want to be a good teacher. And you all need to tell me how to be so that I can do my best job. Do you think you can help me out?"

Everybody wanted to answer this question. Hands shot up all over the room. They were still accustomed to raising their hands. After writing the sentence stem "A good teacher . . . " up on the board, I readied myself once again to cluster their answers. The answers came quickly—apparently, they were anxious to go outside for recess.

A good teacher . . .

- likes kids
- plays sometimes and works hard
- was good when they were little
- goes to church sometimes
- is interesting
- uses good manners in the classroom
- teaches a lot
- has to show that he or she can be good
- listens to kids

After writing their answers on the board, I thanked them for their responses and asked one final question. "Of all the qualities of a good teacher, which one is the most important?" It didn't take long for them to decide. It was unanimous. Most of all, a good teacher . . . had to like kids.

Now that we were finally finished, it was time to go outside. Trying to be a good teacher, I puckered my lips in and out, swayed my body to and fro, and with my arms held at my sides, flapped my hands like little fins.

Jose picked it up right away, "You're pretending to be like Swimmy!"

Swimming towards the back door of our classroom, I said, "That's right Jose! Now will all you other little fish hiding in the dark shade of rocks and weeds,' venture forth, so that you can come with me to explore all the wonderful things out in the sea?"

Slowly and quietly, all the little fish got up out of their seats and swam to the back door. They organized themselves, swimming close together, each in their own place. With me acting like Swimmy, we exited the classroom and swam together, like one giant fish, towards our designated area of the playground sea. We had become an organized school of fish.

Dream School

I felt pretty good about what had happened with the reading of *Swimmy* and the questions afterwards. It was fun. Engaging my students in a participative process of designing our classroom in an attempt to generate more responsible, empowered, and fulfilled human beings capable of contributing positively to a democratic society, made me feel a little more productive. But there was still much work to be done.

The next day, we talked about why we do the kinds of things we do in the classroom. We talked about rules, why we walk in lines, why we learn math, why we read, why we sit quietly and raise our hand and wait to be called on before shouting out answers, why we refrain from taking something out of another person's hands, why we don't push people, why we don't hit people—why, why, why.

The kids all knew the reasons why. Unfortunately, just because they were able to cognitively identify why we did things didn't mean their behavior would match their rationalizations. Something more than a rational element was needed. Maybe an attractive, shared vision would help.

To attempt to form this shared vision, I chose to apply a systems design methodology to the emerging democratic learning community within my classroom. With this systems design methodology, the principal protagonists (my students) who would benefit from the designed human activity system would be actively involved in the design process through my services as a process facilitator rather than content expert.

It all sounds pretty complicated, but it wasn't really. What I did was to take my class on an imaginary trip in a make-believe rocket ship to our very own, unique "Dream School." "Takeoff" would consist of a few open-ended, guided-imagery exercises in order to facilitate my students "jumping out" of the existing system to dream anew. I had hopes of providing an experience that would tap into their imaginations so that together we could plunge deeply into our collective unconscious. Once there—who knows?—maybe a shared archetypal vision of the ideal learning environment would emerge. Wouldn't that be cool?!

When our rocket ship landed, when the guided imagery exercise was over, we could then set out to manifest our new Dream School right there in Watts! Even if we couldn't make it happen, we could have fun trying. And, at least we would have something that we could dream about, and hope for. Our Dream School could be absolutely anyway we wanted it to be! We could learn about and do anything that we wanted, as long as it didn't hurt anybody. We were only limited by our imaginations. The difficulties would come, of course, when we were finished forming our shared vision. That's when it would become my job to help my students, as much as possible, apply their shared vision to the learning that we were doing within our classroom. Naturally, we would have to deal with the constraints of the existing system, but we would handle those unfortunate realities when they arose.

The first series of questions employed by the systems design methodology addressed the mission or purpose of our idealized school. This series would beg the all too neglected questions of "Why are we going to school?" or "What is the purpose of education?" Try asking most teachers or administrators that question and see how they answer. I'll bet not many have taken the time to question the taken-for-granted assumptions that shape their view of pedagogy and education.

I wanted to see how my students would answer the question. Would the answers be profound or profane? Could the children give us any insight as to the future of education, or would they offer answers that were simply a regurgitation of old, outdated ideas?

So, I wrote the question on the board, encouraged them to remember their vision of their idealized Dream School, and asked, "What are you going to school for?"

- to learn
- to feel good
- to be happy
- to do stuff
- to be smart
- to be an angel
- to tell the truth
- to be honest
- to be a person that studies a lot
- to do the right thing
- to be able to help others
- to read
- to graduate and get a job

After they were finished providing all their answers, I asked them to write all the responses on a piece of paper. When they finished copying all the responses, I asked them to number, from 1 to 3, the three most important answers given.

The number one answer was "to be happy"! The second most important answer was "to be able to help others." What wise, profound-thinking little people they were! And the third most important answer was "to learn." Not once did the answers "to do well on our standardized tests" or "to help us make money" get picked as one of the top three answers! I wondered how the profane-thinking educational establishment would've reacted to that. Probably that my students were nothing more that just a bunch of silly, romantic kids living in a dream world.

Then came the second question in the series. That's when the real magic began. I wanted to know, "If everybody in the community went to your school, your Dream School, what would you want people and the community around you to be like? What would families be like? What would other children be like? What would your friends be like? What would you be like?"

At first, the question went nowhere. They didn't know what to answer. They weren't responding at all. They were stuck and I was getting frustrated. How could I help them realize how important this was? How could I awaken their consciousness about the myriad social problems in their neighborhood and engage them actively in the solving of those problems? How could I motivate them to dream of, or idealize, something new for themselves, their family, and their neighborhood? And if that did finally happened, how could I help them move towards this idea by attempting to manifest their shared vision right here in their own community?

That's when I got real. "Hey, remember, this school that we're designing is your school. It's your Dream School. You can do anything with it that you want. It can be any way you want." I paused for a moment and then continued, "Let's imagine that everyone in Watts went to *your* school. How would they be? Would they be the same way that they are today? Think about it. Most people know Watts to be the worst neighborhood in Los Angeles! And it's your neighborhood! Do you like it this way? I mean come on! Look around! There's graffiti on the walls, trash everywhere, drug dealers all over the place, gangs, people getting into fights and arrested all the time, drive-by shootings! Now, do you want it to stay this way? Because, it doesn't have to, you know. You can help change it. Everyone, and I mean everyone, goes to school. Everyone in your neighborhood has gone to school at one time in their life. They may have dropped out, but they must have gone to school for a while at least. Now, if they went to your school, well, how would they be? How would you be? How would you like your neighborhood to be?" Finally the answers came:

- We would care about each other.
- People would be able to take care of themselves.
- People would be nice to each other.
- We would all be unique.
- We would keep the environment clean.
- People would be happy.
- We would be healthy.
- We would respect each other.
- We'd all be smart and intelligent.
- We would be special.
- There would be no smoking.

- Nobody would use drugs.
- There would be no violence.
- There would be no guns.
- There would be no pollution.

Now we were getting somewhere. We were beginning to touch the outer edges of the educational moment! The kids were ready—emotionally, psychologically and intellectually—for what we were doing. The intimate questions about what was taking place in their community right outside our classroom door were effectively drawing from their personal experiences.

Like I had secretly hoped, when we completed answering the question, Danyell came up with an idea that helped to determined our direction or, if you will, our sense of participation in a sacred purpose, for the remainder of the year. Still calling me by my last name, "Mr. Gust," she said, "can we make posters of all our answers and hang them out in our neighborhood? We could hang them on poles, on sides of buildings, everywhere. Can we, Mr. Gust?"

Needless to say, I was excited. The rest of the kids were excited, too. Most of them got out of their seats to swarm me at the chalkboard. "Yeah, Mr. Gust, can we? Please!? Can we, Mr. Gust," came the pleading chorus of questions.

"Of course we can!" I shouted back. "I'll get some posterboard and markers and paint and stuff, and you guys can make your posters. Then when you're all finished, I'll laminate them, and then we can go on a walking field trip out in the neighborhood and hang your posters wherever you want!"

Our mission was emerging right before our eyes. My students were becoming purposeful little human beings, flying free in their little rocket ship, utilizing social action means to manifest the design of their school and community.

Meeting Meghan

I met her—well, I really didn't meet her, but I first became acquainted with Meghan at a seminar that I gave for the Teach For America/AmeriCorps USA organization. I was asked by Teach For America to give a professional development to some of their new teachers on how to help enhance their students' self-esteem. Meghan, a fresh recruit in the program, was in the beginning of her first year as a fifth-grade teacher in Compton Unified School District.

Meghan was in the audience, sitting near the back of the room, but, for some strange reason, she stood out from among the others. I wasn't exactly sure why, but it was probably because of her eyes. They were huge! Well, not really huge; it was more like they sort of did something. They seemed to jump out at me the way a young child's eyes did when gazing at something that excites her. *Intense* would be the best way to describe Meghan's eyes. Yeah, that's it—intense.

Anyway, from where I was standing, it was easy to tell that Meghan had the mental capability, courage, childlike innocence, and genuine curiosity to challenge my thoughts and ideas. And I was glad. But for some reason, she kept quiet that day. Maybe it was because my presentation was sound, or maybe the ideas furnished simply weren't worth challenging. Or maybe it was because she was exhausted from teaching all day. I don't know, but, for some reason, I knew she was paying close attention. Her eyes said it all.

Once my presentation was over, when a few of the new teachers gathered around to ask questions, Meghan came up to buy the teacher resource book that I had published on enhancing student self-esteem. Reaching through the crowd of teachers, she quickly passed her check for the proper amount, nodded her head in approval, and promptly departed. I watched her walk out of the room, thinking all the while that she was very much like I would have been if I were attending another teacher's presentation—quiet, somewhat reserved, an observer rather than a total participant, thoughtful, and forever questioning.

Two days later, we met again. I was sitting on the floor, looking at a children's book in the Either-Or-Bookstore in Hermosa Beach. I needed to find some additional resources that would provide ideas for another teacher resource book that I was writing. Typically, not many people entered into that particular area of the bookstore, so when someone invaded what was, at the time, my space, I looked up. It was Meghan. Except, I didn't know for sure who she was. I just knew that I had seen her somewhere before. So I spoke up and gave her what must have appeared to be a total pick-up line, "Hey, haven't I seen you somewhere before?"

Quick to head off any aggressive pursuer, Meghan gave a response that was to be expected, "I don't think so; I just moved here."

Realizing where I had seen her before, I asked, "Wait a minute; I know. You're a Teach For America teacher. Didn't you attend a seminar I gave a couple days ago?"

"Oh yeah," she said, "you're that self-esteem guy."

Great, now I was known as 'the self-esteem guy.' Last thing I wanted. "Well, if you mean that I was the one who gave that seminar on self-esteem, then I guess yeah, you're right. So what brings you in here?" I asked

"Well, I'm planning a multicultural unit and I'm trying to find a book called *People,* by Peter Spier."

"I know that book. It's fantastic. But you won't find it here. Besides, you don't want to buy that book anyway. You can get it at the library. As a matter of fact, I just happen to have it in my apartment, sitting on my living room floor, near my computer. I borrowed it from the library about a week ago."

"You know, I was just at the library. They said someone had checked it out. So you're the one that has it."

"Yep, I'm the culprit. But if you want, you can come to my apartment and borrow it." I realized how this whole conversation could be misconstrued as the ultimate pick-up.

Looking at me somewhat distrustfully, she said, "All right, I guess so."

"Well, let's go then," I said, picking myself up off the floor.

"You mean now?" she asked.

"Yeah now. You want the book, don't ya?"

Meghan and I had both walked to the bookstore, but because I lived about two miles away, we decided to walk the much shorter distance up the hill to her apartment first. When we got there, we jumped in her little red car and drove to my apartment.

Once inside, I gave her the book, and with a huge smile on my face, said, "See, I told you I had the book." She put her hands on her hips and smiled.

"Listen, I know this looks like some kind of pick-up, but since I'm giving you my library book, you've got to give me your phone number so that I can get a hold of you. I want to make sure I can get my book back again. I'd like to avoid having to pay any library fines should you decide to keep the book."

"You don't know if you can trust *me*?"

After Meghan wrote her name and phone number on the Post-it pad sitting on my desk, she thanked me for the book and said good-bye. I wished her luck. She was still in her first year of teaching, and I knew what kind of challenge that offered. For some reason though, I knew Meghan would do just fine.

About a week later, I began to wonder how she was doing with my book. Did she use it yet? Did the kids like it? When was she going to be finished with it? Actually, more than anything, I wanted to get the book on her library card rather than mine. Let her pay the fines should she keep the book past its due date! Grabbing the Post-it note now adhered to the cabinet top of my desk, I gave her a call. We arranged to meet later that night at the library so that she could put the book in her name.

It was then that Meghan and I became friends. Seems the library was a good, neutral place to meet and talk about teacher things. Naturally, being a first-year teacher, Meghan had lots to talk about. We talked for hours about everything from classroom management—a big concern for rookie teachers—to parents, instructional methodology, the lack of materials and supplies, administrative constraints, her recent move to Los Angeles, and, of course, children. As I had figured, Meghan had a keen and inquisitive mind. From our conversation it became apparent that she was going to become a good, healthy buddy, as well as an excellent teacher.

About a week later, I called Meghan to invite her and her friends out for a few beers and to play a couple of games of billiards at Shark's Cove, one of the local bars near her apartment. She accepted the invitation and said that she'd bring along a friend. Once there, we all had a great time. After we had our fill of beer and finally got tired of playing pool, we decided to walk around the corner to Java Man to get a cup of coffee and continue our conversation in a more quiet atmosphere.

About as quickly as Meghan and I became friends, we also became colleagues. Coincidentally, when we first met, I was also looking for a fellow teacher to co-author a couple of teacher resource books that a publisher had contracted me to write. I had just finished writing three other books and, at the time, I was getting tired of working alone. Plus, I didn't enjoy writing all the practical lessons that these pragmatic books provided. I wanted to find someone who would be willing to write the bulk of the practical lessons so that I could focus on the theory that supported and gave direction to it all. I had invited several other teachers to collaborate with me on the books but was unsuccessful. I had all but decided to drop the idea when Meghan came along.

Knowing all the while that I was earnestly looking for someone to work with me on the books, Meghan never said a word to suggest that I ask her. I never considered asking an inexperienced, first-year teacher to co-author the books. Then one day, while we were in the middle of a conversation, the idea came to me. Why not ask Meghan? She would be perfect! True, she was new to teaching, but she was a driver like me and, even though she had a challenging, critically thinking mind, she probably wouldn't argue too much about the content of the book. I could coach her and basically teach her how to write the lessons.

Meghan was a quick learner, and she would get a lot of experience from the opportunity. What a perfect fit!

So I asked. "Hey, you know I've been looking for someone to co-author those books with me, right? And you know that I haven't been able to find anyone, right? Well, I was thinking, how would *you* like to work with me on them?"

"Wow, I'd be honored." She paused, considering the possibility. "Yeah, I'd love to write those books with you."

"Great!" I said. "It'll be a piece of cake."

"But before we get started, I have only one question," Meghan announced.

"What's that?" I asked.

"What's my percentage of the royalties going to be?"

I should've known. Already a challenge. Fortunately, I liked challenges . . . and Meghan.

Their Community?

I kept asking myself why was it only *their* community? My students were supposed to make a difference in *their* community? Why not *our* community? Why did I still perceive the Watts community as *their* community? If I thought of myself as having been called to the teaching profession, then why didn't the call beckon me to the community where my students lived? Why was I living in a community other than Watts? Why was I limiting myself to being a so-called external expert, intervening Monday through Friday, 7:20 AM to 2:40 PM? Why did I perceive myself as not being intimately affected by the consequences of my actions?

Maybe it was time to become more of an equal member, active participant, and beneficiary of the Watts community. Why not share its real-life experience as well as the outrage and joys it may involve? Why not become intimately engaged with the community? If systems design was most pertinent to the community and the greater society, and commitment to implementing it more certain, when consummated by those who serve, utilize, and are affected by the system, then why was I bothering to engage my students with the design of our classroom system when I was not also intimately a part of the system? Was my behavior unethical?

I thought perhaps it would be best if I moved into the Watts community to see what it was really like. I was familiar with the community from my role as teacher and from the media, but I didn't truly *know* the community. I was familiar with it conceptually, as a mental construct, but it wasn't embedded within my personhood. If I moved into the community, then maybe I could come to know and experience Watts as it really was. I would understand what my students, and their families, went through everyday of their lives. Perhaps I could even open up my house to both my students and other members of the community, in order to have a "rubbing of elbows," so to speak, in my living room, where everyone would be on equal ground.

But what kind of commitment would that require? Nobody I knew actually wanted to live in Watts. Everyone, it seemed, wanted to get out. Nobody wanted to go back in. And besides, at the beginning of the school year, I was actually regretting having to go back into the inner city to teach, and now I was thinking of actually moving in?! I had to be nuts. Forget it! I could be a good enough teacher without having to actually live in Watts. It wasn't required by our school system. Nobody could force me to move in.

It kept eating away at me, though. While continuing to work on determining my personal philosophy or worldview, I kept questioning myself and my values as a human being rather than as just a teacher. Was my behavior ethical? Then one day, as I was contemplating all this, I pulled John Dewey's classic *Experience and Education* down from my bookshelf. I purchased the book a long time ago at a used bookstore, for who knows what reason, but had never even cracked it open . . . until then.

Leafing through the pages, I came upon a section that grabbed my interest. I read how the American philosopher, psychologist, and educator believed that the primary responsibility of the teacher was to "know how to utilize the surroundings, physical and social, that exist so as to extract from them all that they have to contribute to building up experiences that are worthwhile." Okay, okay, so I should know how to utilize the environment, but that still didn't mean that I had to move into the community to do so. And let's face it, I *was* still working within a traditional educational system. I really didn't have to face this challenge. I could as Dewey said: "systematically dodge this responsibility. The school environment of desks, blackboards, a small school yard, was supposed to suffice. There was no demand that the teacher should become intimately acquainted with the conditions of the local community, physical, historical, economic, occupational, etc., in order to utilize them as educational resources."

But was *I* a traditional educator? I didn't think so. But would moving into the community support my emerging worldview and corresponding philosophy of education? Well, if I were stuck giving it this much thought, probably so. Besides, Dewey's comment about systematically dodging a responsibility was working its way under my skin. And there must have been a reason for that, too. However, I still needed to think about it before deciding. I needed time to judge whether or not my actions were ethical.

White Man Can't Think

"I've been thinking about it for a long time," I said to my friend Marc as we pedaled along the bike path on the beach. We were on our usual Saturday morning ride, heading south towards Hermosa Beach. It was a warm morning, and the rising sun made the ocean water look extremely clear.

"Thinking about what?" Marc replied.

"Well, I've been thinking about moving into the neighborhood."

"What neighborhood?"

"Watts."

"Watts?!" Marc yelled, nearly running off the bike path onto the sand. "You must be crazy."

"Maybe. I've been thinking about it, though."

"You've got to be kidding!" Marc said, shaking his head. "Sounds to me like you haven't been thinking at all."

Marc and I had been friends for a very long time. He lived with his wife Laura and two boys in a beautiful house in Playa Del Ray. He had two cars, an

$8,000 stereo, mountain bikes, exercise equipment, pool table, televisions, tons of toys and sporting goods for his children—all of the things most conventional families had. The guy loved sports—football, basketball, baseball, hockey, you name it. Marc had always been a very conservative guy—a Wharton Business College graduate, businessman, very smart and practical. The first time I met him, I called him "Computer Chip." I never knew anyone who could store so much information in his head at one time. His memory was fabulous.

Through the years, I got the impression that sometimes Marc thought I was a little crazy. This was obviously one of those times. He asked, "So, what are you going to call this new little 'experiment' of yours?"

"I don't know," I explained. "I didn't much think about what I'd call it. Plus, I'm not sure I'd call it an 'experiment'. It's more like . . . an adventure."

"Another one of your adventures, huh? You want to know what I think? I think you ought to call it, 'White Man Can't Think'. That's what you ought to call it. I always thought you were nuts. Now I'm sure of it. Move into Watts!? Great idea!"

Normally I'd just shrug off Marc's comments, but this time I felt like I had to give him an explanation—more for my sake than his. "Maybe your right, maybe I am nuts. But the truth is, ever since going back to teaching in Watts, I've been thinking about embedding myself directly in the surrounding environment of the school. Something keeps telling me that I will never really be able to understand myself and my students, or effect some positive social change, unless I become fully and actively involved in the community. I've been thinking that if I continue to intervene as some sort of 'outside expert,' I won't be doing much good. Besides, I don't know if it's right to enter my classroom at the start of the day and then leave the community where my students live right after they go home. I don't think it's right to ignore the larger social context of schooling anymore."

Sensing that I was pretty serious about this, Marc sincerely asked, "What do you want to do in Watts?"

"I'm not exactly sure. Learn, I guess. I want to learn about the people, the community, and my students. Maybe that'll make me a better teacher. Plus, I need to learn about myself as well." I didn't attempt to tell Marc about my efforts to discover and articulate my worldview and philosophy of education. That would be too complicated.

Surprisingly, Marc didn't have very much else to say. We spent the remainder of our ride thinking our own thoughts, concentrating on our workout.

When the ride was over, after saying good-bye to Marc and returning to my apartment, my thinking—or as Marc would claim, lack thereof—brought me to considering the idea of cruising the streets around the school in Watts to get a better idea as to whether or not this was a commitment I really wanted to make. And if I did decide to make the move, well, I could also begin my search for an apartment or a house to rent.

After showering, I phoned Meghan and canceled our plans to work on our book for the afternoon. I explained what my real interest was, and to my surprise, she expressed her desire to go along. More than anything, with her intense interest and bachelor's degree in architecture, Meghan wanted to see the famous Watts Towers, the sculptured home of Simon Rodia, an Italian immigrant who settled in Los Angeles in the 1920s. She had been wanting to check out this historical and cultural sight for quite some time. So, that afternoon, after picking up Meghan, we headed out in my Jeep to Watts.

Arriving at the Watts Towers, the first thing we noticed was that the huge structure was surrounded by scaffolding. Apparently, the towers were being repaired or restored in some way. From what we could see, though, it was quite an interesting-looking place. What was more interesting to me, however, was the history of the guy who made this fascinating structure and how he made it.

Simon Rodia was born in Rivatoli, Italy, sometime around 1879. He immigrated with his family to the United States in the 1890s and settled in Pennsylvania. When he became older, Simon moved to the west coast and worked as a construction worker and tile setter in rock quarries, logging, and railroad camps. In 1921 Simon purchased the little triangular-shaped lot on 107th Street and began to create his masterpiece. He called it "Nuestro Pueblo," or "Our Town" in English. For 33 long years, this guy, after putting in a hard day at work, came home and, without the help of any machines, equipment, scaffolding, bolts, rivets, welds, or drawing board designs, built the nine major structures of the Watts Towers. Construction work in his day had to be tough, and from the look of it, he didn't have an easy time of constructing his towers either—especially if he didn't have any tools or scaffolding to use! The tallest structure was ninety-nine and a half feet tall! Plus, he worked alone on these towers, using only a tile setter's simple tools and a window washer's belt and buckle. You had to admire the guy.

After Meghan was satisfied with her view and critique of the towers, we went to the Dr. Martin Luther King, Jr., Shopping Center on 103rd and Central. While there, we stopped, so that Meghan could go in the Payless Shoe Store—she was badly in need of a new pair of shoes. While she went in the store to buy a pair of aerobic shoes, I stayed outside to read the memorial plaque of Dr. King's "I Have A Dream" speech.

Just as I finished reading, Meghan came out to proudly display her new shoes. "And I only paid twenty dollars!" she exclaimed.

"Congratulations," I said. "Now let's get back in the Jeep. I want to cruise up and down the streets near my school to see what type of apartments or houses might be available to rent."

As we were driving on a street with fairly decent looking homes, I noticed about ten kids playing in someone's front yard. I drove by slowly and thought I saw one of my students in the small crowd. It was Donnell. I stopped the Jeep and backed up. When Meghan zipped down her window, Donnell yelled out, "Mr. Gust," and then he and the rest of the kids walked up to the car.

Even though my students were given explicit permission to call me "John" instead of "Mr. Gust," they never did. Probably out of habit or convention, they continued to call me by my formal sur name under all circumstances. I didn't mind really. Didn't consider it something to spend any time correcting. Maybe it kept me in a position of authority and my students subjugated in some small way, but then again, maybe it was just comfortable and safe for them, as small children, to know that "Mr. Gust," and whatever that meant, was around.

"What are you doin' on this side of town?" asked Donnell.

"We're just cruising the neighborhood, looking around," I said, without wanting to disclose too much.

We engaged in some small talk for awhile, said good-bye, and drove off. Some of the kids tried to race alongside the Jeep on their bikes as we drove down the street.

The next day, Sunday, Meghan and I decided to get together to work on our book. But, with thoughts about moving into Watts still racing around in my head, I felt compelled to go back to the neighborhood. Part of the reason was because I had been reading the children's book *Maniac Magee*, by Jerry Spinelli. Meghan and I were considering using the book to support a thematic unit on "respect" for our own teacher resource book on multicultural education. *Maniac Magee* was the winner of the 1991 Newbery Medal and was, by my personal standards, an excellent book.

In the story, a young white boy, who's parents had died in a train wreck subsequently moves in with his crazy aunt and uncle, until he has enough of their dysfunctional behavior and decides to run away. On his travels, Maniac eventually settles down in a segregated neighborhood where the whites live on one side of town and the Blacks on the other. The dividing line between the two factions is a busy street.

As the story develops, Maniac spends time on both sides of the street. Sometimes, he stays with the Blacks on one side, and other times, he lives with the whites on the other. Sometimes, however, because of the discrimination and prejudices that he encounters—from both sides—Maniac lives on his own.

As I read the book, trying to decide if Meghan and I should use it for our work, I marveled at how coincidental it was that I was reading it then, while also giving thought to moving into the predominately African American and Latino Watts community. I was interested in the book's themes of respect and ending discrimination and prejudice.

With the book's themes in mind, I gave Meghan a few instructions to continue working on our book, picked up a couple of chocolate chip cookies and an apple, and set out for Watts in my Jeep in search of a new place to rent.

Driving down the freeway, I thought about my living arrangement in Manhattan Beach. The rent in my apartment-with-a-view was way too high, and I was getting sick and tired of all the gourmet coffee shops, BMWs, Mercedes, Saabs, surfers, the beach, bike rides on the strand, and breath-taking sunsets. Sure I was! Maybe Marc was right; maybe I really couldn't think. Aside from my high rent, why would I want to leave this neighborhood?

As I entered Watts alone, just like the first time I drove into the neighborhood prior to taking the job, I became scared all over again. Trying to calm down, I asked myself out loud, "What do I have to be afraid of?" And then, as if in answer to my question, I started receiving threatening stares from the Black men hanging around. Once, as I was driving down 107th street for the second time, a group of men standing in the housing development's parking lot, began shouting something at me. I didn't quite hear, or understand, what they were saying, because I was driving too fast, but it sure did scare me—a lot.

After that, I made a point not to drive down 107th Street again. I didn't want to start any trouble. Continuing to drive on some of the other streets nearby, I began to feel that perhaps I really wouldn't be welcome here. Maybe there was no "table of brotherhood," as it said on the memorial plaque in Dr. Martin Luther King, Jr., Shopping Center nearby, that I would be able to sit down to in this neighborhood. And maybe all my wishful thinking wouldn't make it so. Maybe we never would be able to watch "little black boys and black girls . . . join hands with little white boys and little white girls as sisters and brothers." Maybe we never would "be able to work together; to play together; to struggle together; to go to jail together; to stand up for freedom together knowing that we will be free one day." Maybe Dr. King's dream would have to wait.

I knew how Maniac Magee must have felt in Jerry Spinelli's book when he decided to forget about the trouble of trying to bring people together. Perhaps, more accurately, I was more of a megalo*maniac* than anything else. To most people, people like my friend Marc, I *was* obsessed with doing something extravagant, grand, unrealistic, or just plain crazy. To him, I was just some overly purposeful guy with a crazy, romantic notion of martyring myself. Maybe Marc was right; maybe this white man really couldn't think.

Visiting Victor

After the encounter with all the boisterous men in the parking lot, it became apparent that if I were going to move into Watts, I would need a liaison, someone to introduce me to people in the community. A white guy moving into a Black and Latino neighborhood could be threatening, raise much suspicion, and might even create a reaction—a reaction for which I didn't want to be responsible. I thought about the people available at school, and the first person that came to mind was Ms. Johnson. Ms. Johnson was a first-grade teacher and a well-respected, very popular woman who had lived in the area most of her life. And she and her children went to school at Compton Avenue.

At lunch time one day, I walked into her room and asked, "Ms. Johnson, have you ever known any white men who have lived in the area around our school before?"

"No. Why? You thinking about moving in?" she asked in return.

"Actually, yeah I was. But, I don't want to create any fuss or anything, so I thought I should ask around first. You know, talk about it with some people and all."

"Well, it's probably a good idea—you talking about it with people and all. You don't want to just jump right in. 'Sliding in' gracefully might be a little better. You know who you should talk to is Anthony, one of the campus aides. He still lives around here. He could probably give you some good advice."

After talking with Ms. Johnson, one way or another, word got out around school that I was considering moving into the neighborhood. The following day while getting some things out of my mailbox in the front office, Mrs. Ruiz grabbed me by the arm and took me aside. Looking at me as if I were a crazy man, she asked, "Is it true? Are you thinking of moving close to school?"

"Yeah, I thought it might be a good thing to do."

To say the least, she wasn't supportive. Mrs. Ruiz was a good woman, motherly and caring, but not too courageous. She tried to warn me of all the changes that I would experience, of the dangers involved. She also told me that she had taken the liberty of talking to Anthony before I had a chance. Apparently, Anthony also expressed his concerns for my safety. As Mrs. Ruiz told me later, Anthony thought that I might be in for a little trouble.

Several days later, during recess, I found Anthony out on the schoolyard, watching the kids. Actually, Anthony found me. This was a relief, really, because quite honestly, I didn't know how to introduce the idea, considering all the delicate issues that might arise. We talked, or rather Anthony listened and I talked.

Stumbling my way through expressing my concerns, I didn't want to give Anthony—or anyone else—the impression that I had something to be afraid of, that I thought everyone living in the area was to be feared. I certainly didn't want to be accused of stereotyping anyone. More importantly, I didn't want anyone thinking that my intentions were to shape things up, to fix things, to show people how to live, to teach them new ways of behavior—in general, to be their savior, their "great white hope," so to speak. I wanted everyone to understand that I was coming in as a learner. Fortunately, Anthony was a good listener. I believed he felt my sincerity.

Anthony told me about the people living in the area and about what I could expect. "It's a good idea that you talk with as many people as you can before moving in, because if you don't, their gonna think you're 'The Man.'"

"'The Man'?" I asked.

"Yeah. You know, the police," he explained.

By the time we finished talking, it appeared as though Anthony had changed his mind about my moving in. He thought it was a good idea. I felt relieved.

The next person that I decided to speak with was Victor. Ms. Johnson and Anthony both thought it would be a good idea. Victor was Danyell's step-father. Danyell, one of my more popular students, had a brightness that shined mostly when she was doing any kind of oral language activity. She was a loud student who knew how to use her voice. Anytime we read a book in a choral reading activity, or anytime we did any explicit, systematic phonics, it was usually Danyell's voice that could be heard above all the others. She loved to read and talk.

Victor, I discovered, was a very popular guy in the neighborhood. He also had quite a reputation. We first met when he visited our classroom during the first Parent–Teacher Conference of the year. He was a big guy and, as Danyell proudly explained, an occasional minor league football player. From time to time, Victor played for the L. A. Mustangs. When Victor brought his large, jovial self into the classroom with Danyell, I knew we would hit it off right away. In some ways, I felt Victor and I were, well, kindred souls of sorts. And now, after hearing Anthony's and Ms. Johnson's reports about Victor, it became apparent that if I were going to become a part of the neighborhood, I was going to need his help.

Later, after speaking with Anthony, as I was dismissing the class for the day, I took Danyell aside and asked her to tell her father that I would be giving him a phone call later that night. I didn't want Danyell to think that she was getting in any kind of trouble, so I told her that I wanted to talk with her father because I was hoping that he would show me around the neighborhood.

When I called Victor later that night, we hit it off right away. First, I had to tell him to quit calling me Mr. Gust, and then I told him about my plans to move near the school. I expressed my concerns and asked him if he could show me around a bit and maybe introduce me to a few people to help alleviate their suspicions, if they had any. He thought it was a good idea. I was relieved. As we concluded our conversation, we made plans to meet at his house the next day, Friday, after school at 4:00, so that he could give me a tour of the neighborhood and introduce me to as many people as possible.

The following afternoon, instead of meeting Victor at his house, he unexpectedly arrived at school shortly after the kids were dismissed for the day. Apparently, he got off work early and decided to come by the school. He sent

Danyell to the classroom where I was still busy working, getting things in order for the following week. Not wanting to be bothered by anyone at the time, I had the door closed. Danyell knocked on the door hard, and when I opened it, she pranced in with who I assumed was her younger sister. "My daddy's outside waiting for you, Mr. Gust."

"He is? Already?" I responded.

"Yeah, he just got off work. He's still wearing his work clothes," Danyell added.

"And who's this cute little girl? Is she your sister?"

"Yep," answered Danyell.

"And what's your name, little girl?" I asked.

With a sheepish little smile on her face, she shyly and quietly offered, "Brianna."

Knowing Victor was waiting, I quickly finished my work in the classroom, shut off the lights, and closed the door. When Danyell, Brianna, and I made our way outside, Victor was on the playground, talking with Anthony. He was dressed in workboots, jeans, a dirty sweatshirt, and a mesh fluorescent vest. He looked like a cityworker—which he actually was at the time. When the girls and I finally approached Victor and Anthony, we shook hands, said good-bye to Anthony, and started walking towards the parking lot. While walking, we agreed to go to their house first and then take our drive around the neighborhood from there.

"Mr. Gust, can I ride along with you in your Jeep?" pleaded Danyell.

"Its all right with me, as long as you have permission from your father.

Without hesitation, Victor nodded his head and said, "It's awright."

Most of my students asked if they could ride in my Jeep, so this must have been a real treat for Danyell.

When I started the Jeep, the radio came on with the volume full-blast. That morning I had obviously been listening to something I liked. Danyell looked over at me with her little nose all curled up, looking as if she had just smelled something pungent, and said, "This is the kind of music you listen to?"

"Yeah," I said, trying to tease her a little. "Don't you like it?"

She looked at me and shook her head furiously in disbelief. I like classic rock; Danyell, on the other hand likes, well . . . you know the stuff. I call it "Boom Boom Music." Personally, I can only stomach that stuff for very brief periods. A sign of my maturing age, I guess.

As the music boomed over the stereo system, much to Danyell's displeasure, I sang along just to mess with her a little. "You mean you don't know this song!" I shouted. "I can't believe it."

After I turned down the volume to a tolerable level, Danyell asked, "Mr. Gust, can you drive fast?"

"Well, I can, but I don't think that's a very good idea right now, Danyell."

"You might have to though, Mr. Gust, 'cause my daddy drives real fast."

Danyell was right! I had to blow through a couple of lights just to keep up with him!

When we arrived at their house, we went in right away. While Victor apologized for the mess, Danyell grabbed me by the hand and dragged me to her bedroom. Brianna quietly followed behind. Apparently, Danyell wanted to show me her domain. As terrible as it sounds, the first thing I noticed were the two unmade twin beds and the filthy walls. I guess kids in all neighborhoods liked to put their hands all over the walls. For some reason, however, I didn't notice anything else besides the unmade beds and the dirty walls. When I was a child, I thought, my obsessively clean mother would've reprimanded me strongly if my room had looked like this.

After I thanked Danyell for showing me her room, we made our way to the kitchen, where Victor was taking off his vest, sorting through the mail, and checking to see if he had any telephone messages. Once Victor was finished, we exited through the front door.

"You better pull your car off the street, Mr. Gust," offered Victor.

After pulling my car onto his driveway, stashing my briefcase under the carpet, and locking my doors, Victor closed the large steel gate behind my car and locked it tight. High crime rates in the area called for extra precautions, I guessed.

While Victor and I got in the front seat of his station wagon, a giggly Danyell and Brianna climbed in the back. With Victor driving, we were back near the school in no time at all.

Unfortunately, it was an uncharacteristically rainy day for Los Angeles, so there really weren't that many people out on the streets, hanging around the Hacienda Village housing development.

"My mom and my wife's mom both live here in Hacienda," Victor explained. "It's not bad really; my mom's only paying $40 a month."

"You serious? That's all? Why's that?" I asked.

"Because she's Section 8, and been living here so long. My mother-in-law's paying a little more, though," he added.

I wasn't exactly sure what "Section 8" meant, but I figured it was some sort of government-assigned status, probably based on income, that enabled his mother to rent property at an enormous discount.

"You know, my brothers and I all grew up in Hacienda. My mother raised all five of us alone."

"What about your father?" I asked.

"We're pretty close, but I don't see too much of him," he explained.

The more Victor talked, and the more I listened, the more comfortable he became. Eventually, he stopped calling me Mr. Gust. I found it easy to listen to

Victor. He was a great storyteller. As much as possible, I tried not to judge any of Victor's tales. Instead, I did my best to feel the humor, sadness, excitement, and tragedy he must have felt.

He shared the story of when he first went to high school: "John, when I was in high school, I got kicked out of Locke for fighting. A couple a gang members wanted me to join their gang, but I wouldn't do it, so I got into a fight with one of them. I stabbed the son-of-a-bitch in the neck with a pencil. I lasted three days at Locke. They expelled me after that."

He told me his version of the recent Rodney King/L. A. Riots: "Oh, man John. The riots were a lot of fun. The cops totally cleared out. We was having a great time. I looted a couple of stores, but mostly I wanted money. So my friend, this guy who had a tow truck, we hooked it up to an ATM and pulled it out of the wall. Money was everywhere, John. You should've seen it. People were grabbing at everything. I got 7,000 bucks. Man, we had fun."

He told me the story about his two motorcycle accidents on 107th Street: "People always race down that street. The first time I was racing was with a friend. We bumped bikes goin' about 110. I fell and got my foot caught in one of the tires. The bike must've pulled me on my back at least a hundred feet. I wasn't wearin' a helmet. It scraped all the skin off my back. I was in a coma for three weeks, but I got out of it without any broken bones. The second time, my brakes went out. I was going way too fast to stop. I flew across Compton Avenue and almost got hit by a school bus. My front tire hit the curb and sent me flying over the bike through Markham's (the middle school) fence."

He also shared the story about how his drug-dealing friend gave him an old '54 Chevy, which he later showed to me in his garage after our trip concluded. He told me how he got his reputation as a good guy by buying ice cream and shoes for some of the neighborhood kids, and about how he would push some of the bigger guys off the basketball court to give the little kids a chance to play for a while. He told me how he never once used drugs or had a drink of alcohol. And he told me, and I could definitely tell, how much he loved the kids in his neighborhood.

As much as I tried to avoid it, however, I did feel a twinge of judgment arise occasionally as Victor told his stories. I couldn't help but cringe inside when I heard about how much "fun" he had during the riots.

My mind drifted back to my personal memories of the riot. I remembered how much anger and hatred were expressed back then. I remembered going to the school in South-Central where I was teaching at the time following the riots. The whole school was uncharacteristically quiet and dismal. The gas station directly across from the front door of the school was burned to the ground. Kids told stories about how they saw people getting shot, how they talked to soldiers standing in the alleyways in back of their houses. I remembered the fear in their faces and how they each wanted to hold the little puppy that I had brought into school, as if to bring some comfort, some sense of innocence back into their lives. I remembered the principal finally asking me to take the little puppy out of the school, and the kids groaning when I pried it out of their arms.

I certainly didn't want to hold anything against Victor, and I surely didn't want to end our friendship just because he did some things that I, coming from my background, wouldn't have done. At the time, in spite of my judgments, I thought Victor's stories were interesting and exciting, and, surprisingly, I felt something beginning to bring us together. Something similar, in a way, to the feeling that I got from the handshakes that I received from men in the area; slow, firm, yet gentle, with a slightly prolonged hold, almost as if there were a reluctance to let go.

Looking at Victor's two daughters in the back seat of the car, as my tour was coming to an end, it became apparent that I didn't want to let go of this experience either. Obviously, an abundance of contradictions and dilemmas was going to accompany my move into this neighborhood. Brianna was sound asleep, but Danyell's bright, beautiful face was pressed up against the cold, rain-dropped window, staring out at the gloomy, ugly street below.

House for Rent

I had to find a fairly decent place to live if I were going to move into Watts. I didn't want to live in a dump, but I did want to live as close to school as possible. Ideally, I wanted to be able to walk to and from school with my students. So, I spent a lot of time driving around the neighborhood, writing down the phone numbers of houses and apartments for rent. There weren't very many places to choose from. While driving alone, I continued to notice all the looks I received. Occasionally, someone would yell something at me as I drove by, but, as Victor, Anthony, and Ms. Johnson at school explained, most of the young men that yelled at me probably thought I was "The Man."

A couple of times, I thought about getting out of my car to introduce myself, to explain that they had nothing to worry about, that I wasn't the police. But then I would convince myself to stay in the car for fear of getting mugged. When I told Victor about all the guys yelling at me as I drove by and my desires to get out of the car, he said that if I did, they would probably just run away. They were most likely selling drugs and didn't want to get caught.

Then one day after school, while touring the neighborhood around the school in my Jeep, I saw a house on 107th Street that looked promising. It was just three short blocks from school! I wrote down the phone number from the "For Rent" sign on a Manhattan Beach dry cleaners receipt that was resting in my

Jeep's console. When I returned to my apartment in Manhattan Beach, I dialed the number on the receipt right away. I spoke with the landlord, Elidio, on the phone and he agreed to meet me at the house the following day after school.

The next day, I drove to the house and waited patiently in my Jeep for the landlord to show. Elidio pulled up in a big pick-up truck ten minutes later. His wife and daughter were in the car with him. Elidio got out of the truck and introduced himself while his wife and daughter remained seated.

Right away, I knew the place would be perfect. The weathered front of the bright yellow, Craftsman-style house had a large, raised cement porch. I imagined several chairs or a bench, bats, balls, bikes, and assorted other toys resting there. After Elidio unlocked several locks on the two heavy front doors, we went into the house. As soon as we entered, I realized that the interior looked nothing like the exterior. From the front door we had a grand view of the living and dining rooms. The walls were covered with a beautiful dark wood that gave off a very deep, homey, and grounded feeling. I could picture a rocking chair with a throw draped over the back, a standing lamp, and a framed painting in the corner near the built-in bookshelf. My couch, coffee table, chair, television, and potted plants would be placed on the other side of the room.

After walking into the dining area, where the dark wood continued to cover the walls, I noticed a hutch with leaded windows built into the back wall. Overhead, the ceiling was adorned with big, thick, heavy wooden beams. A large round table with at least six chairs could easily fit in the middle of the room. It would be really great if I could get people from the neighborhood to sit around the table for discussions on various important topics.

These two living areas would be the public domains of the house. Children would use the front area, while the adults could sit around the table. I would oscillate back and forth from the bench on the porch outside, to the rocking chair in the living room area, to the round table in the dining area, making sure everybody was happy.

The kitchen was very large. It certainly had enough room for my kitchen cart right in the middle in front of the stove. I could imagine large meals being cooked for any get-togethers. Along the side of the living room, dining room, and kitchen were the three bedrooms. These would be the private areas of the house. The front bedroom would be large enough to serve as my office and bedroom. I imagined my bed towards the rear of the room and my desk placed towards the front. This was where I would do my work. The other two bedrooms would hopefully be filled by other teachers or people who also wanted to live in the neighborhood.

Overall, the house was a total mess. The windows were covered with dirty, ripped bed sheets, the carpeted floors were filthy, the walls were badly in need of paint and repair. The whole house smelled musty, sort of like wet, dirty dogs. Actually, the house needed a lot of repair and cleaning, but I didn't mind. During my first viewing of the house, I was beginning to look forward to fixing it up and making it feel all homey and comfortable. The house certainly had a lot of potential.

After looking over the inside of the house thoroughly, Elidio and I went outside so that I could check out the back of the house. It was then that I realized that this large house also had a "back house." We walked through the gate and proceeded to make our way up the driveway, dodging all the land mines. Dog shit was everywhere! A young pit bull was chained up to the shack or garage in the back of the lot. As we got close to the structure, the pit bull started to whimper and whine—he was looking for attention.

I don't think anyone was expecting us, because the next odor that was brought to my attention was the sweet smell of marijuana. I said out loud to Elidio, "Smells like someone's having a little party." Just then, two young Black men with glassy eyes scurried out of the shack. They were in their teens or, at most, in their early twenties. Elidio had no idea what I was talking about, so I explained to him that I could smell the pot that they had been smoking.

I didn't want to scare the two young men, so I nodded in their direction, said, "Hey," and continued looking at the house and the yard. Mostly, I wanted to see how secure the house was from the outside. Some of the windows were without bars and I was slightly concerned. I told Elidio that I wasn't happy about the lack of security, and if I were going to move in, he had to put bars over the back windows.

After I was finished looking the house over, Elidio and I talked about rent, utilities, and all the other important details. Luckily for me, Elidio significantly lowered the amount of rent that he was asking for. I figured that if I looked disinterested enough and didn't make a decision, I might get him to lower the price down even more. Knowing that I was a teacher working at the elementary school three blocks away seemed to make him understand that I would be a reliable tenant. It became obvious that Elidio wanted to rent the place as soon as possible, so I told him that I would think about it and give him a call.

The next day, a very rainy and gloomy afternoon, I visited the house again. This time I met Meghan out in front. She knew that I had been giving thought to the idea of asking a couple of Teach For America teachers to move into the neighborhood with me, and, of course, being a Teach For America teacher herself, Meghan was considering the possibility. While we were parked outside, talking about the prospects, the back house tenant, who I later discovered was nicknamed Pee Wee, walked out from the backyard with five other Black men. He was being pulled along by two large, adult pit bulls on one thick leather leash. From the leather leash, two heavy chains branched out to the spiked collars around each dog's neck. One of the dogs was a female who had obviously just had a litter, and the other was an aggressive, and horny, male.

Pee Wee was very angry. He started yelling at me about the landlord and the condition of the house. "Fuck this, fuck that, muther fuck this, muther fuck that." He accused Elidio of being racist and went on and on, ranting and raving about his living conditions. As he did, the male pit bull jumped up on the female and started humping away. The female, who must have become tired of the male's constant pursuit, snapped away fiercely. The male dog just kept coming though, and the two of them chomped away at each other while rising up on their hind legs. Pee Wee had to punch the two dogs on their noses with his fist to get them to stop. Pee Wee's companions looked on, somewhat amused and embarrassed.

Meghan and I thought the whole affair was rather peculiar. I had to laugh inside. I was concerned that with Pee Wee and his pit bulls living in the back house, I wouldn't be able to get a good night's rest if I were to move in. Plus, I doubted that I would be able to get anyone else to move in to share the rent and the experience. Who in their right mind would want to live there with Pee Wee and his crazy dogs in back? I looked at Meghan, as she quietly sat in her car through all of this, and she just shrugged her shoulders. Oh well, I wanted a true-to-life situation, and I was surely going to get it if I moved into this place.

While finalizing all my arrangements with Elidio the next day, Donnell showed up at the house to check things out. That kid was all over the neighborhood, all the time. There wasn't a single time when I was visiting the neighborhood that Donnell wasn't around. Fortunately, I was happy about that. Donnell was one of the sweetest little boys that I ever had the pleasure of teaching. Earlier that day he apologized to me when I accidentally bumped my elbow into his head as he was trying to get to the front of the line. Donnell was the line leader, and he was supposed to be at the front of the line. I bumped my elbow into him, and he apologized? His manners were unusual among my students. What a terrific kid.

When I left my landlord so that he could continue working on all the repairs that I was demanding—mostly bars on all the windows and doors—I went outside to talk with Donnell. Unexpectedly, Meghan pulled up in her car. Knowing that I would be there working out the final arrangements with Elidio, Meghan decided to drop by after work unannounced. I was happy to see her. Just then, Donnell's sister and cousin also arrived. This was quickly becoming quite a gathering. After Donnell introduced Meghan and me to his sister and cousin, he asked, "What are you doin' here, Mr. Gust?"

"I'm moving in," I explained

"You're movin' in?!" they exclaimed in unison.

"Yep, right here."

"Why?" Donnell's sister asked.

"Because I want to live close to my students and the school."

Just then Donnell saw his mother down the street and said, "There go my mama." As he started off on his bike, Donnell yelled, "Mr. Gust, come meet my mama."

Meghan and I rode in the Jeep while Donnell and his companions raced down the sidewalk on their bikes. When we reached Donnell's apartment, his mother Rita invited us in. We walked into the apartment, and the first thing I noticed was the smell of fresh paint. The walls had just been painted. I was glad to see that the whole apartment was very clean. Over the years, I found that many of the homes of my students were quite messy. First thing Donnell did was to rush into his bedroom. In seconds he came out showing us his new toy. It was this crazy contraption with bright lights and a siren. I couldn't really make out what it was, but it looked like some kind of spaceship or something.

More concerned with my surroundings and what his mother was saying, I replied, "Cool." After that brief acknowledgment, Donnell promptly returned his toy to its proper place.

Rita invited Meghan and me to have a seat on the sofa. After talking about Donnell and his school work, I explained to Rita that I was moving into the yellow house down the block. If she was surprised, she sure didn't show it. I expressed my concerns about the neighborhood and the dangers I might face.

Rita tried to assure me that there was basically nothing to worry about. According to her, the neighborhood was quite a safe place, contrary to what everyone else on the "outside" was saying. She also assured me that because I was a teacher and that I was here to help the children, people, or more specifically, gangsters would probably leave me alone. The only thing she did tell me was that I shouldn't allow the people who came to the door to do any work around the house. They would try to steal things. She also told me not to buy any of the "hot stuff" that people would eventually try to sell me.

"You mean people come around at night trying to sell food?" I asked. I thought "hot stuff" was the chili powder that the kids were always eating.

Meghan and Rita laughed together as they tried to explain that what she really meant was that people would try to sell stolen merchandise. Trying not to look like a fool, I said, "I know stolen things are called 'hot,' but I thought you meant that stuff kids eat."

After Rita and Meghan were done having their laugh at my expense, I asked again about the gang element in the neighborhood. Even though Rita had assured me that I had nothing to worry about, I wanted to know about how the gangs' presence was influencing my students. Rita told us about the time that Donnell, young pup that he was, tried to join a gang. "When I found out he was trying to join a gang, I stripped him down naked and whipped him." Mama would have none of that. And Donnell obviously found out what it was like to cross Mama. Seems as though Mama had reason enough to watch out for Donnell. Mama didn't want Donnell to get mixed up like daddy. You see, Daddy was in jail.

Moving In

Moving to Watts took at least a week. There was a lot of closure and new beginnings that came with moving. Saying good-bye to the old neighborhood and being welcomed to the new one took a little time. I had old utilities to turn off and new ones to turn on. Plus, I had been moving small things for the entire week before my big moving weekend, by putting as much as I could inside my Jeep every morning before work. I'd get to the new house about a half hour before work and unload everything in the Jeep and then make my way to my classroom. By the end of the week, this was beginning to tire me out.

When driving on 107th Street in the U-Haul with my friend Bill early Saturday morning, I passed by Donnell and a few of his friends. As usual, they were on their bikes, roaming the neighborhood. I beeped the horn and said, "Hey," out the window. They waved and quickly turned around to follow the truck back towards the house. Donnell was accompanied by Ricardo, Darnell, and Lavell. Lavell and Darnell were students at Compton Avenue and Ricardo attended Markham Jr. High across the street. I knew an opportunity when I saw one, so I asked the boys if they wouldn't mind helping Bill and me take a few things off the truck. They were ready to go, so we started.

Ricardo was the most helpful; he worked the whole time. Lavell was also very useful, but he didn't stay with the job as long or as intensely as did Ricardo. As for Donnell and Darnell, well, they were second and third graders, so what could I expect? As soon as they found the slightly opened box with a few toys in it, their attention diverted. The boys took out a small rubber football and started throwing it around out in front of the house. After playing with the football for a while, they also found the two dumbbells that were packed away. This time all the boys took out the dumbbells and tested their strength. I didn't mind; as a matter of fact, I found it quite comforting that the boys were there playing on my front porch as I originally had imagined when first checking out the house with my landlord. I was hoping that I would have some companions in the way of students, and this certainly set a precedent.

After we finished moving everything out of the truck, I was treated to a "neighborly" visit from an energetic guy pushing a beat-up shopping cart. He introduced himself as "Floyd the Recycle Man." Floyd was one of the regular fixtures of the neighborhood. One of those resourceful hard-up guys who spends his time walking through the neighborhood pushing a shopping cart full of bottles, aluminum cans, newspapers, cardboard, and other recyclable materials.

On my way to work, I'd see those guys pushing their carts in alleys, picking through the plastic trash bins the L. A. Resource Program provided. At other times, I'd see them on the corner of 107th and Compton, trading in recyclables for cash at the private recycling center directly behind the liquor store. In the de-industrialized economy of South Central Los Angeles, recycling trash was, for some, the only way to survive. That day, Floyd had a big ugly piece of flowered carpet sitting on top of his old shopping cart. He pulled it down off his cart, unrolled it on my front lawn, and said, "Nice carpet, huh? You want it? Make me an offer."

"That thing's ugly. I hate old-fashioned flowered carpets," I said.

"Yeah, maybe you do, but your lady will like it," he said. "You'll find some use for it."

I looked at him, with his stocking cap pulled over his head and his old raggedy clothes, and thought to myself, "What do I really want to do here? Do I want to shut this guy out right from the beginning, or do I want to make a new friend?"

"Name your price!" he shouted as I stood there looking down at the carpet.

"Okay, I'll give ya ten for it," I said.

"It's yours," he said.

Realizing that I probably offered him a whole lot more than he would've expected, I reached into the truck, took out my wallet, and gave him the two fives I had left.

"Thanks," he said. "You want me to help you take it into the house."

Rolling it up and hoisting it over my shoulder, I said, "That's okay, I can handle it." I really didn't want him in my house because I still had all my valuables exposed, including my computer.

"Hey Floyd, before you leave, do me a favor, will ya?" I asked.

"Sure what is it."

"Keep your eyes open for an old rocking chair and a floor lamp. If they're good, maybe I'll buy them, too."

The next day, I found an old office chair and a contemporary lamp on my front porch. I hated them both, so I left them outside. That evening, he stopped by, and gave me his sales pitch. Figuring I could use it somewhere, I wound up buying the chair for two bucks.

The landlord Elidio and his son were also there that moving day to finish putting all the bars on the windows and doors. He was also there to turn on the hot water heater. Elidio, my friend Bill, the boys, and I went through the house to the backyard to take a look at the water heater. Bill, a plumber by trade, was the best person to have around for turning on a hot water heater.

When we reached the backyard, we were greeted by four little pit bull pups. The pups belonged to Pee Wee, of course. The boys seemed pleased that the pups were there. While Bill and Elidio attended to the water heater, I had fun watching the boys play and frolic with the pups. The boys looked like little pups themselves, especially when the big daddy pit bull came charging around the corner. Startled by his aggressiveness, the boys scurried into the back doorway of the house like a litter of pups, pushing and shoving trying to maneuver into a safer position around the protective opening of their den. All the big pit bull wanted to do was to join in on the fun, but the boys were too frightened to notice. I laughed and laughed, then squatted down calling to the big male pit bull. It came to me quickly and licked my hand. Big ferocious dog.

Done with our work on the water heater, Bill, the kids, and I went around to the front of the house again. Bill and I spent a little time throwing around the football with the Donnell and the others and then went inside to tidy up a bit before returning the truck. I wanted to make sure my computer was well covered. When moving it from the truck to the house, I made certain that the computer was covered with a blanket so that anyone who might have been watching nearby wouldn't be able to tell exactly what it was. I was still very suspicious of the neighborhood and, besides, why give the local thieves any incentive to break in. I made doubly sure the computer was covered, threw a few small things over it for camouflage, locked the front door, and then jumped into the truck with Bill.

Later that evening, when I returned to spend my first night in the house, I could have sworn that the computer had been slightly exposed. The blanket seemed to have particularly come off the computer. Could somebody have gotten in already? Slightly nervous about what I saw, I went around the house, checking all the doors and windows. But I was too tired to worry about it too much, so I took a long, hot shower and went directly to bed. As soon as my head hit the pillow, I was sound asleep.

Waking up early the next morning, I skipped breakfast and returned to Manhattan Beach to help my friend Marc, his wife, and two boys move into their new home. Coincidentally, they had purchased a new home right around the corner from my old apartment. Marc was hoping to be neighbors, but I obviously had another calling. Some time ago, I had promised Marc that I would help him move when the time came. Unfortunately, his move coincided with my move.

Marc and his family had a lot more things to move than I did, so moving them took much longer that second day. By the end of two full, hard days of moving, I was totally exhausted.

After I was done helping Marc move all of his family's things, I went back to my old apartment to gather up a few more things before heading back to Watts. While at my old apartment, because the phone, fortunately, wasn't scheduled to be turned off until the following day, I received a phone call from an old friend who had just flown in from out of town. Jas was in town for the day and wanted to get together for a quick drink before heading back to Chicago.

Jas arrived at my empty apartment just as I was getting dressed after taking a quick shower. After helping me load up my Jeep with the few things that I had left, we went to the Hennessy's restaurant in Manhattan Beach for a beer. When our beers arrived, I told him of my plans to move to Watts.

"Watts?! You're moving to Watts?" he yelled. Always amazed at people's reactions, Jas, like everyone else, thought I was nuts.

We argued over my decision for a while, but when Jas realized that changing my mind was a hopeless cause, he gave up. "Listen Jas," I said, "I need to go back to Watts to finish unloading that stuff in my Jeep. And when I'm done with that, I want to go to Jordan High School to watch the filming of a video. Supposedly, a music video is being filmed there. From what I heard, its being directed by the same man who also directed the movie "'Cool Runnings.' If you want, you're more than welcome to come along."

Jas, inquisitive young guy that he was, couldn't pass up this opportunity to see what I was up to, so he decided to come along. "Yeah, sure, I'll go. I just gotta see this."

When we got to the house, I showed Jas around. After he had a chance to see the living and dining rooms, we made our way back to the kitchen. When I turned on the kitchen light, I noticed that the things that I placed up against the back door looked as if they had been moved. "Jesus Christ, Jas, I didn't leave those things like that!"

Immediately, I got scared and ran towards my bedroom. Sliding open the big heavy wooden door and jumping into the room, I looked to see if my computer were still there. Luckily it was. Breathing a sigh of relief, I wondered if I were just seeing things. "Maybe I'm imagining things, Jas, but I could've sworn that I put the kitchen stool with the glass bowl on top of it firmly up against the back door of the kitchen."

When I walked out of my bedroom, Jas looked at me with concern and shook his head in disbelief. "I was afraid that someone might have taken my computer," I said, "but it's still there. Maybe I'm getting paranoid."

As I said this, my eyes scanned the living room looking for anything else that might have been taken. I noticed that the TV was still in its place. I looked around at my Sony music box and noticed that it was still there. Then quickly, I looked back to the TV cart and realized that my VCR was gone! I ran over to the TV cart, looked behind it in disbelief, and said, "Fuck! It's gone! They took my VCR!" My fears were confirmed; someone had been in my house earlier that day.

I felt as if I had been raped—a victim, totally helpless and powerless. Wanting to cover up and protect myself, I reached for the handle of my front door to close and lock it, but was shocked and disgusted by the big, ugly cockroach crawling on the handle. Pulling back my hand, I kicked the door and squished the roach. A chill went through my body. I wanted to run out of that place as fast as I could. I wanted to pack all of my things and head back to my old apartment in Manhattan Beach. I absolutely could not stand roaches! Ugh! I didn't know which was worse—the stolen VCR or the disgusting, filthy roach on my door handle.

Gathering my wits, and before leaving for Jordan High School, I decided to have a little talk with Pee Wee. I asked him to come into the house, showed him where I thought the thieves might have gotten in and asked him if he saw anything. He acted dumb. "You know," I said, "right now I don't know how good an idea it is bringing you into my house to show you where the thieves might have come in. As far as I'm concerned, I can't trust anybody around here yet." Pee Wee turned his body to look me straight in the eye. I did the same with him. "For all I know," I continued, "it could've been you who got in here and stole my VCR."

We stood there toe to toe, about a foot away from each other due to the small amount of space in the pantry, staring at each other. Without blinking, Pee Wee said, "Yeah, you're right not to trust anybody right now."

Turns out that my hunch was right. I discovered later, that at one time, my landlord gave Pee Wee a copy of the key that opened the back door. Elidio told me that Pee Wee gave the key back to him. But sly guy Pee Wee more than likely made a copy of the key and waited for the right opportunity to find his way back into the house. Much later, one of the guys in the neighborhood, who I had become friendly with, explained that he overheard Pee Wee bragging about his little exploits. As I suspected, Pee Wee *did* get into my house to steal my VCR . . . and three coffee cans full of coins. I didn't even know the change was missing!

At the time of the incident, I decided not to call the police. I thought it would be best not to draw any attention to the affair. By bringing the police in on it, I would just be exacerbating the problem and inviting some other form of retribution that Pee Wee, or anyone else involved, might provide. So the issue died right there, right away. I was only out $180 and some change. You could say that it was my "initiation" to the neighborhood.

Knowing that there was nothing that I could, or would, do about the situation at the time, Jas and I locked up the house as best we could and headed off for Jordan High School to watch the filming of the music video. I figured that the thieves probably wouldn't be back. If they wanted anything more, they would have taken it earlier that day. But just to be sure, I picked up my computer and found a better hiding spot in a closet with a lock on it in the back bedroom.

That night after we left Jordan High School, I said good-bye to Jas, watched him drive off, and locked the door. Totally exhausted and spent, I went to bed immediately. Unfortunately, however, Pee Wee's little pit bull pups spent the night rummaging through the garbage right below my bedroom window. I tried banging on the window to scare them away, and I thought about going outside and throwing a few rocks. Or even telling Pee Wee to do something about it. But I was way too tired to get up. I fell asleep with the little scavengers still going at it.

Monday morning, while riding my bike to school, someone called out from across the street. It was James' mother. I slowed my bike down and pulled off the street to join her on the sidewalk. When I did, she promptly informed me that James had forgotten to bring his homework to school. Handing over her son's homework, I discovered that James also lied to her about how much homework he had. I commented that three pages were missing.

Later, when all my students were entering the room to begin the day, I pulled James aside to ask him about his homework. "Hey, James, I saw your mother on my ride into school this morning. She gave me your homework."

He walked over to my desk to collect the page that I was holding. Before I would let him take the sheet from my hand, I said, "I guess you forgot to tell your mother that we all agreed that we were going to complete three more pages of homework, huh?"

Looking down at the floor, James nodded his head. "Maybe you can finish your homework at recess time, huh?" Living on the same street as James was going to have its advantages.

With all the homework collected, we all settled down and started our morning discussions. Our first topic was roaches. I told the kids the story about my house getting broken into and then about the roach on my door handle. Everyone in the class knew just about everything there was to know about roaches. When I asked, "Who here has ever had roaches in their house?" everyone raised their hand. The rest of our morning discussion centered around what do to get rid of the disgusting little creatures. All the kids shared their stories about roaches.

Karen knew all about the subject and offered the best advice to keep them away. She explained that I needed to clean up the house real good, to throw away all my garbage right away, to make sure to wash my dishes as soon as I was finished eating, to make sure I didn't leave any food out, to put roach hotels all over the house, and finally to "bomb" the house with those spray cans that I could buy at Food-4-Less. I thanked Karen for her sound advice and began our agreed-upon lessons for the day.

When the final bell of the day rang, I left right with the kids. I pushed my bike out of the room, down the hall, while the class walked towards the exit. I wanted to ride through the Hacienda Village housing development rather than take the long route home on the main streets, but I didn't want to ride alone. I might have been crazy, but I wasn't stupid—I wanted some protection. I recruited Donnell to ride along with me. So, once we were off school premises, Donnell hopped up on my handlebars and I peddled for home.

On our ride through Hacienda Village, a few kids jogged alongside the bike for a while. They all wanted rides. "Sorry guys, it's Donnell's turn today. You're gonna have to catch me another day."

Luckily, I didn't run into any trouble, but I did notice that we received a ton of stares. It wasn't often that a white man rode a bike through their neighborhood.

After dropping Donnell off at home, I went home, picked up my Jeep, and drove directly to Gus Hardware at the end of my block on Central Avenue. I wanted to buy a wide variety of locks, deadbolts, and horizontal blinds for all the windows at the house. Dirty, smelly sheets were still covering the windows. They must have been hanging there the whole time the last tenant was there. I wanted to get them off the windows as soon as possible. I was hoping that getting rid of the sheets would help to alleviate some the musty smell inside.

When I returned home, a young Jr. High School student, Larry, who lived three houses away offered to help me bring my supplies into the house. While we unloaded the Jeep, Larry filled me in about the history of the house. Turns out the house was a Taj Mahal of sorts. When the house was vacant, all kinds of bandits came into the house through the back door to drink, smoke pot, and do drugs. Larry even showed me how they got into the house. They came through the back doors after they climbed up on top of the roof and jumped down in the little space that separated the front house from the back house. I was moving into an old crack house! Good thing Elidio barred the door and windows back there. Hopefully, that would keep any other thieves and crackheads out.

After Larry went on his way, I proceeded to put all the locks and deadbolts on the back door of the kitchen that lead to the pantry in the back of the house, on my bedroom door, and on the extra door in the bathroom that lead to the pantry in the back of the house. I went berserk with locks. Finished with the locks, I called my landlord Elidio, told him what had happened, and demanded that he get over here right away to make sure he finished putting the bars on the windows and doors. By the time the house was secured, it had a grand total of twenty-three locks, not including the bars over the doors and windows.

While getting ready to leave for work the following morning, I followed Karen's advice and set off the four roach bombs that were also bought at Gus

Hardware. I placed one in the kitchen, another in the living room, the third in my bedroom, and the last one in the bathroom. Prior to that, I also set out two packages of roach motels in strategic locations throughout the house. The thought of roaches crawling anywhere in my house made the hair on the back of my neck stand up. I had no plans of letting those disgusting roaches get the best of me.

Meeting the Neighbors

Mrs. Wear and Mrs. Watkins were the very first neighbors that I met. After noticing the two elderly ladies busy talking on the sidewalk right in front of my house, I stepped outside to introduce myself. Walking with my hand outstretched, down my porch steps to where the two ladies were standing, I opened up the conversation, "Hi. My name's John and I'm a teacher over at Compton Avenue. I just moved here to be close to my students and a part of their community."

While shaking my hand, the smiling Mrs. Wear and Mrs. Watkins explained that they had been living in the neighborhood for over fifty years. Mrs. Wear, who lived a few houses down the block, was a widow living with her daughter. She was quick to inform me that she was herself a teacher at one time. She had taught in the Los Angeles Unified School District for thirty years at several schools in the South Central area.

Mrs. Watkins, who lived directly across the street, didn't focus on herself at all, but rather chose to talk about her family instead. She had a daughter who was an assistant principal at nearby Budlong Avenue Elementary School, a son who was a detective with the Los Angeles Police Department, and a husband who was retired from his work with the Los Angeles Department of Water and Power. From what she told me, Los Angeles couldn't have asked for better citizens than the Watkins family.

When the introductions were over, we talked extensively about the schools in the local area. Mostly, we talked about Compton Avenue Elementary, and how the two of them used to be very involved with the school, especially when their children were enrolled. I listened as they explained how the years changed things for Compton Avenue. The very opinionated Mrs. Wear seemed to think that it was due to the new principal and the lack of a PTA at the school.

"Yeah," I said. "I've been wondering why we don't have an active PTA. Why is that?"

"It's because the principal doesn't want people from the community getting involved. That's why," offered Mrs. Wear. Mrs. Watkins nodded her head in agreement.

Finally, after a little more chitchat, I told Mrs. Watkins that I looked forward to meeting her husband, then said good-bye to the two ladies and went back into the house. Mrs. Wear and Mrs. Watkins continued the conversation they were having before my arrival.

The following day, I had the pleasure of meeting Mr. Watkins. He was standing on his front porch watering his lawn, so I went over and introduced myself. When we got to talking, I found Mr. Watkins to be an extremely friendly and honorable gentleman. Everything about the old guy reminded me of my deceased grandfather—the way he talked and the things he talked about, the way he held himself, his bad back, the way he dressed, the old fashioned values that he personified and advocated, the way he appeared in the context of his house and yard, even the way he stood on his front porch, surveying the street. I knew right away that I was going to like him.

When Mr. Watkins moved to the neighborhood back in 1944, most of the street was a prairie. In those days, he would often leave his front door unlocked at night. He could even leave his kids' toys and bikes on the front lawn. In times past, he knew every one of the people living on the street and could trust all of them. Now, however, Mr. Watkins had few acquaintances in the neighborhood. Not so much because people weren't friendly, but because, nowadays, he chose not to associate with most of the people living there. He was visibly disgusted with the way the neighborhood had gone steadily downhill in recent years. According to Mr. Watkins, it all started when the housing developments infiltrated the neighborhood. "Make sure you watch out for yourself after the first and fifth of every month. That's when the people living in projects get their welfare checks. Things around here get crazy then. I won't even go shopping then."

Mr. Watkins said that the house I was renting was originally located on 55th and Vermont. It was moved to 107th Street by an elderly couple who had lived there until they passed away years ago. Knowing that the condition of the house was less than desirable, Mr. Watkins explained that the elderly couple kept the house up before it changed ownership numerous times after their departures.

A few days later, I met up with Mr. and Mrs. Watkins' daughter. Actually, I became reacquainted with her. Some time ago, I presented a seminar at the Los Angeles Teacher's Center, and Donna Wilson, now the assistant principal at Budlong Avenue School, was once of the participants. Talk about coincidences! When I saw Mrs. Wilson drive up in her shiny red Corvette to visit with her parents, I was just getting ready to borrow her father's lawnmower to cut my grass. We politely said hello and soon began talking about my return to the school district and her relatively new position as assistant principal at Budlong.

After catching up with what we had been doing since the seminar, I said good-bye to Donna and wheeled Mr. Watkins' lawnmower across the street to cut my grass. Just then, a tall, stooped-over man wearing an old hat came out of the house next to mine. It was Harvey, my other next-door neighbor.

Beforehand, Mr. Watkins had warned me about Harvey: "Harvey used to be a big-time drug addict. You name it, he's been on it. Harvey's just a lazy good-for-nothing nobody! Never worked a day in his life. Won't even cut his own grass. Watches his eighty-year-old father do it for him. His daughter's nothing more than a prostitute. I won't have anything to do with 'em. I do enough for him; as a tax payer, I pay for his SSI relief; that's enough."

Harvey seemed like a nice-enough guy to me, though. I didn't have any beef with him. With a cigarette dangling out of his mouth, he introduced himself and said that if I needed any help with anything, I could come knocking on his door. We didn't talk much, but it was nice of him to come over. I almost wished that Mr. Watkins didn't tell me anything about Harvey beforehand. It would have made my impression of him all that much better.

Just as I was finishing up with the lawn, another neighbor, Big Larry, stopped by. Big Larry, who lived a couple of houses down, had a loud booming voice, huge smile, and gigantic belly. His son, Little Larry, who really wasn't so little, was the one who introduced me to the colorful history of my house. When Big Larry walked by, his introduction quickly turned into a business proposition. Promptly informing me that he washed and detailed cars, he said I could bring my car around anytime, and he'd "do me up real good." I thanked him for the offer and told him I'd give it some thought. That said, Big Larry went on his way down the sidewalk.

While returning the lawnmower, I asked Mr. Watkins whether or not it would be a good idea to let Larry clean and detail my Jeep. Mr. Watkins said, "I let him do my car once and he did a terrible job; left wax in all the cracks, tires still dirty, a terrible job. I wouldn't let him do my car anymore after that."

The following day, Big Lar' came over to the house to borrow some money. Said he needed to get a prescription filled. Said he had a bad back and needed to take a lot of medication in order to get out of bed in the morning. I didn't have any reason not to believe him, and he did only asked to borrow two dollars, so I gave it to him. As he took the two dollars out of my hand, I wished him luck on his back. He said thanks and quickly took off towards Compton Avenue to the drug store . . . I presumed.

A few days later, Larry's youngest son, Brian, knocked on my door. After I invited him in, he asked if I had any Tylenol for his father's bad back. While explaining that I didn't have any, which was true, because I never had a need for pain killers, I couldn't help but notice that he had a patch of ringworm on his forehead. This was no ordinary small, dime-sized patch. Brian looked terrible. His ringworm dominated the whole left side of his forehead and was progressing far into his hairline! How could Big Larry and his wife have allowed such a thing to happen to their child? It couldn't have been a matter of money that kept them from taking care of it. All they had to do was to take Brian to the Watts Health Center around the corner and they'd fix him right up, no charge.

Realizing that something had to be done quickly, I took Brian into the bathroom and made him wash his hands and forehead real good. Then I took the tube of athlete's foot medicine that I had in the medicine cabinet and gave it to him. It had the same ingredients that any ringworm medicine would, so I made him put it all over his forehead and rub it in real good. With the white cream still showing, I sent Brian on his way, making him promise to bring back the empty tube once he was done with it. I wanted to make sure he would use it all.

The following day, I told Mr. Watkins about my encounter with Brian. Mr. Watkins explained that Brian's mother and father had been on drugs when they had him. Little Brian spent four months in the hospital before he was released—a drug baby.

Now, I knew a few kids who were called "drug babies" by the teachers at school, but having had the chance to see Brian and the way his parents neglected him was another thing altogether. Somewhat surprisingly, it made me think of all our challenges in the classroom.

At the time, as a teacher, I felt that taking Brian into my home and teaching him how to use medicine to take care of the large ringworm growth spreading on the side of his forehead was deemed my responsibility. Did this task fit my job description? No. Did it need to be done? By me? Maybe, maybe not. Perhaps, it was just the neighborly thing to do. Teacher? Neighbor? It all seemed to be coming together.

Saturday Morning Cartoons

Lying on the couch, enjoying the morning paper and a hot cup of coffee on Saturday morning, I heard a very soft knock at the front door. Picking myself up off the couch, I walked to the door, looked outside, and saw Jamal motioning to James to, "Come on!" James was a little too shy to come knocking, but Jamal certainly seemed bold enough. Happy to see the two boys, I opened the door and invited them in. James brought in his bike and leaned it up against the wall. They looked around, not exactly sure what to do, so I asked, "You guys want some cereal?" The cute little guys nodded their heads rapidly in unison.

I walked into the kitchen, with James and Jamal following closely behind, and pulled out the two boxes of cereal—Captain Crunch and Honey Bunches of Oats. "Which one do you guys want?" I asked.

They both pointed to the box of Captain Crunch, so I filled up two big bowls and before pouring the milk asked, "You guys want a banana to go with your cereal?"

Jamal said, "Yes, please." James shook his head no.

After I cut up Jamal's banana and poured the milk for both boys, we walked back to the front room. "You boys want to watch some cartoons?" I asked.

Again they nodded yes. I turned on the TV and sat back down on the couch to continue reading the paper. The boys sat down on the floor directly in front of the TV. "Conan the Destroyer" was on. I got the biggest kick watching the two of them slurping away at their cereal while also giggling anytime any one of the bad guys was sliced in half by the powerful sweep of Conan's sword.

When the show was over, the boys got up on their own, took their cereal bowls back to the kitchen and placed them in the sink. I was impressed. When they returned from the kitchen, I asked, "You boys want to draw something?"

Again the nodding. I told them where they could find the Crayola Magic Markers on the shelf in the dining room. I didn't have any construction paper, so I went into my office and pulled out a couple of sheets of paper from my printer. The boys were happy with the supplies. Jamal drew his mother a picture, and James drew one for me. He drew me sitting in my Jeep in front of my new home. I loved it.

"James, this is great. I'm going to hang it up on my refrigerator." I walked into the kitchen, with James and Jamal following, pulled off one of the seashell magnets that I had put there for such an occasion, and posted James' drawing right smack-dab in the middle.

Jamal, much in need of a little recognition of his own, skipped back to the living room and drew another picture, just for me. When he was done, I hung his drawing up on my refrigerator, making as big a deal out of his work as I did for James.

Standing in the kitchen, admiring their work, I asked the boys, "You guys want to read a book?"

Of course, they nodded! So I showed them where they could find the books. Together they chose *The Little Engine That Could*, by Watty Piper—one of my favorites.

"Jamal can read, you know, Mr. Gust," James declared.

"Really?" I said, sounding surprised. Jamal was in the first grade.

Looking up at me with his clear eyes, Jamal nodded his head to let me know that what his brother said was right.

"We can both take turns reading the book out loud," James continued.

"Okay, let's hear ya," I replied.

They both had me fooled for a while, but eventually I caught on. James was ever so quietly telling Jamal the words to read. They were lying on the floor, while I was on the couch. From where they were, I couldn't hear too well at first, but when I eventually had to lean over to help them with a word—indignantly—I could hear James patiently helping his younger brother. It was the sweetest thing. Here they were, two of the toughest boys in school, yet in an intimate moment away from the social atmosphere of the school they were capable of being ever so gentle with one another. I admired James for the way he was with Jamal. I don't think I was ever so gentle, patient, or caring with my younger brother.

When the boys finished the book and the little blue engine had made it over the top of the mountain to bring the toys and good food to all the little boys and girls on the other side, Jamal let out a big "Hooray," just like in the book. James, not wanting to appear to be too sweet, said a subdued, "Yay."

This was, by far, the best Saturday morning that I had had in a long time. I always loved watching cartoons with my brother when I was just a boy. We'd grab our cereal, run downstairs to the family room, wrap ourselves in blankets, and watch cartoons for hours before Mom got up to make us do our Saturday chores. I missed those innocent, lazy Saturday mornings. The morning with James and Jamal was the closest that I had come to those comforting feelings of long ago. Thanks for the memories, boys!

Our Social Action Field Trip

All of our social action posters (the ones Danyell suggested we make of the children's responses to the first series of questions posed in the systems design methodology) were complete. The slogan, artwork, and laminating were all in place. Now all we had to do was to go out into the neighborhood to post them.

Before setting off, however, we had a long conversation about what we were about to do. We talked about how we would act, what we would say to people as we walked along the way, and how we would keep safe, considering the possible dangers we faced. Some of the kids were concerned.

James said that what we were doing—"putting posters up, telling people to stop using drugs and guns, to keep the environment clean, to love your neighbor, is a total waste of time." For James, the problems he experienced daily were permanent and pervasive. Hope was, at times, far away for James.

In response, the creative, hopeful Danyell stood up, put her hands on her hips, shook her head, and yelled back at him, "Hey, it's a start! And it's better than just giving up and doing nothing!"

I was a little concerned for James, especially when I heard what had happened to him recently. He was almost shot by one of the local gangs! Over the weekend, while he was playing in the alley in back of his apartment, the Hacienda Village Boys had a little "scuffle" with someone. Luckily, James got away without being hit. I was quickly becoming afraid that with all the gang influences around him, James might become one of them before too long.

Knowing that there was nothing I could do about it at the time, I began taking care of getting our field trip permission slips in order. They were all signed and accounted for, so we set off with our posters. Our plan was to post our artwork throughout the Hacienda Village housing development right across the street from our school. I felt pretty comfortable with our plan.

As we began our walk, the first thing we noticed—even before getting off campus—was the fresh graffiti on the front wall of our school's auditorium. A tagger had apparently climbed on top of the awning that extends over the front door of the auditorium to write the message. It was the most prominent wall of our school. We decided to post Lakima's poster on the telephone pole directly in front of the tagged wall. It said, "Keep Our Environment Clean."

I led the class across the street and went directly into the busiest part of Hacienda Village. We wanted to distribute our posters throughout the entire housing community, so we restricted our posting to telephone poles only. We were all over the place, hanging up our posters, greeting people, taking photographs, and having a great time. Karen wanted to hold my hand as we walked. She was a little scared.

After hanging quite a few posters, we walked to the western-most end of Hacienda Village. This was a section that I had never been to before. Donnell informed us that this was where his uncle was shot. I hoped we wouldn't encounter any violence there that day. Unexpectedly, at least for me, we happened upon a large playground. Feeling rather generous and relaxed, I suggested that the kids romp on the play equipment for a while. I was surprised when their reaction to my suggestion was less than positive, "Eeew! No way! Not there!"

That's when I took a closer look. What I noticed was an old broken-down, litter-infested playground area that looked like it hadn't been used in years. Garbage and large piles of cut grass were scattered all throughout the area. The play equipment was horrendous. The monkey bars were bent—a car obviously had plowed into it. There was also a rusting slide ladder with no slide attached, a crooked and graffiti-covered round-about, and an eight-seat swing set that had only two working seats.

As I stood there looking at the dilapidated playground, I immediately thought of Meghan. She had a degree in architecture and also had experience designing and building children's playgrounds. She and I were applying social action approaches towards the multicultural education lessons that we were writing in our resource book, but architecture was her true passion and specialty. Maybe we could team up to redesign and rebuild this playground!

But, according to my emerging philosophy, this should be a student-generated social action project, fostered through dialogue, not teacher directives; so how was I going to help my students become aware of the possibility of changing things right here in our community? How could I get them to think about improving our community by completely renovating this playground?

They were totally accustomed to run-down, dilapidated playgrounds such as this. How were they going to envision something new and better if they had never been exposed to anything better? They may never have had an opportunity to see, let alone play, on a playground with clean, shiny, new, functional equipment! And, if I did expose them to something better, wouldn't I also be saying that what they had wasn't good enough. Still though, their original reaction prompted me to believe that they really weren't happy with the condition of this playground.

That's when I asked, "What do you think of this playground? Do you like it?"

"NO!" they shouted in unison.

"Do you think we ought to do something about it? Do you think we could make it better?"

"Yeah! We could make it a lot better," Danyell exclaimed.

Grabbing Danyell to give her a shoulder hug against my hip, I said, "I think so, too. Maybe we will." Then, attempting to enroll the others and build consensus, I asked, "Does anyone else think it's a good idea to help make this playground look better?"

"I do," said Donnell, tugging on my shirt.

"Yeah," said everyone else.

"We could get rid of all this garbage and stuff," said Angela. "And maybe we could change some of the rides."

"Good idea, Angela!" I said. We had consensus; they all wanted to be involved, so with Angela's suggestions in mind, we started our walk back to school, talking about the possibilities. The kids had a lot of good ideas.

That afternoon, when I got home after school, I phoned Meghan and told her about the playground. She immediately signed on. I was so thankful that she was such a "can do" person.

So there it was, finally, some tangible, real-life purpose to my work in the classroom. Now all I had to do was figure out how and where to get funding for such a project, and to convince the Housing Authority of the City of Los Angeles, which managed this housing community, to allow a group of elementary students to design and build a new playground. I was sure that would be no easy task.

"Hello Officer"

It was Friday afternoon around 3:00. Finally, the end of what felt like the longest week of my teaching career. I rode my bike to school that day, so, of course, I had to ride back home. Usually, I chose to steer my bike south on Compton Avenue to 107th Street. Riding this way allowed me to travel on the busy streets. I could ride hard and fast and avoid having to talk to anyone. I received all kinds of looks along the way, but still nobody said anything. This afternoon, however, I decided to ride through the busiest part of Hacienda Village.

When I took this route once before, I rode with Donnell on my handle bars. Having Donnell on my handle bars felt good because he was like my protective shield. I didn't want to use him negatively; it was just that I knew people would identify Donnell and associate me with him. Unfortunately, this time Donnell wasn't around, so I had to ride alone. Luckily, however, Little Larry, my next door neighbor, was walking on the path. I tried to talk with Larry as I rode alongside.

Larry opened up and started telling me about the model cars that he built at home. He explained how he built a total of sixteen and how he sold each one for around $15. I told him that I'd like to buy one, but mostly I was just interested in holding our conversation, hoping to use Larry as part of my protection for this ride home.

At one point, Larry said to me, "Why don't you just make your own models?" I don't think Larry felt much like talking that day. Maybe he knew that I was using him—using him to help me get through the hot spot that I was eventually going to face. As it turned out, my bike was going too fast for Larry's trudging walk, so I gradually left him behind.

Saying good-bye to Larry, I turned to watch where I was headed. Immediately, I noticed several very large Black men about sixty yards away. Continuing to peddle, I mumbled, "Oh, boy here we go." I was a little nervous, and maybe even a little scared, but I kept peddling nonetheless.

It became obvious that the men standing there also noticed me. They seemed to be closing in on the sidewalk that I was riding on. Then, as my peddling became slower and slower, just as my fears were starting to peak, another Black man came out of his housing unit. "Hey!" he shouted. "You're pretty brave to be riding through here without your vest on."

Assuming that he meant the bullet proof vest that police officers usually wore, I replied, "Yeah, either that, or pretty stupid."

He laughed and watched me continue on my way. I was glad that he laughed because it helped to take the edge off. I was lucky, too, because the other men at the end of the path heard the exchange. The group of men looked directly at me and someone started to say something. I couldn't make out what was said, though. It was as if I were in a daze trying to get a grip of the situation. Something inside made me feel that I had better be completely honest and as confrontational as I felt they were going to be, or else I might find myself in a whole lot of trouble.

When I reached the group of men, I stopped riding, got off my bike, and introduced myself. Explaining that I was a teacher at Compton Avenue School, I put out my hand and asked the man standing closest to me what his name was. Grabbing my hand to shake it, he told me his name. Unfortunately, I couldn't hear what he said. He said it loud and clear, but I was still contained within my daze of fear. Still, even though I *was* scared, I was capable of assessing whether or not I had to defend myself—and, surprisingly, I was very aware of our handshake.

I made a deliberate, concerted effort to continue shaking his hand as long as he was willing to continue shaking mine. Standing there holding his hand, with the others nearby, we slowly and carefully checked each other out. As far as shakes go, the hold and the accompanying glare were pretty long. It seemed as though everything were moving in slow motion. From the look in his eyes, I got a sense that this guy was definitely someone to keep *my* eyes on.

Releasing our grip, I turned and shook hands with a man who had a very friendly smile. He was taller than the first man, and also a lot less angry looking. He had very kind, smiling eyes. I felt comfortable with him. The third man was the largest of the three. Except we didn't shake hands because he was standing too far back and obviously didn't want to get any closer. He also didn't want to make too much eye contact either. I said, "Hi," and he simply nodded his head and turned away. I didn't think he trusted me.

Feeling a need to explain myself, I said, "I'm teaching over at Compton Avenue. I just moved into the area so I could be close to the school."

The first man, while pretending to shoot a basketball, said, "Now that you're living in the area, I guess you'll be coming over to the gym."

"Yeah? You've got a gym around here?" I nervously asked.

"Yep," he said, nodding his head.

"I'm not much good at basketball," I said, shrugging my shoulders. "But I do like to lift weights." Then thinking that if I quickly dropped a name I might be able to build a little more trust, I asked, "Hey, do you guys know Victor Cole?"

"Yeah, he's my brother," the first man said.

"He's your brother? You know, he told me his brothers were living here in Hacienda," I said. "His daughter Danyell is in my classroom. Victor showed me around when I was first thinking of moving in. He said we could play basketball around here."

Then diverting the conversation entirely, Victor's brother angrily said, "You know, if a cop came by here right now, he'd jump out of his car, pull out his gun, and have us up against the wall."

Knowing that this was no time to dodge the issue, I asked, "Why, because I'm white and you're Black and he'd think you were doing something to me?"

"Yep," he answered.

I didn't say anything. Instead, I kept looking at him, almost shrugging my shoulders. I didn't make any excuses, didn't apologize. I listened, let him know that I understood what he was talking about, gave him the impression that I knew that that was the way things were, and that there wasn't much any of us could do about it. We both knew that was the truth.

The tall friendly man with the smiling eyes broke the silence, "You know, you're gonna find that there's a lot of nice people around here, too. Most of what you hear on TV is the bad stuff, but there's a lot of good things going on, too."

"That's what I've been finding out," I said. "What's your name again? I'm sorry but I didn't quite hear you the first time."

"Guy," he said.

While I was talking to Guy, slowly, quietly, slyly, Victor's brother made his way to my backside to where the other Black man was standing. For a moment, I thought that the two men actually left and went on their way, but when I instinctively turned around to check, I was surprised to find that they were both still standing there looking me over. It was almost as if they had circled their prey in order to keep an eye on it, to size it up, to check it for any concealed defenses. I was only wearing my backpack, so they had to nothing to worry about. On the other hand, maybe they wanted to know what was inside of it.

I felt it was time to be moving on, so I said thanks and nodded my head good-bye. In return, they all nodded back. I hopped back on my bike and continued pedaling down the sidewalk. When I finally reached the southern perimeter of Hacienda Village, there were two more Black men walking towards the sidewalk. These two looked a little less threatening than the first three. Then again, I may have started becoming accustomed to the situation. The first and friendlier looking of the two men shouted out, "Hello, officer."

"Hi," I said while circling around on my bike. "But I'm not a police officer. I'm a teacher over at Compton Avenue Elementary."

"Yeah, sure ya are," he said, smiling back.

As I rode off towards home, I thought about what Victor's brother had said about how any cop driving by would have gotten out of the squad car and pulled out his gun just because I was talking with three Black men. I thought about how the other guy naturally assumed I was a cop, just because I was a white man in his neighborhood.

How unfortunate it was that my friend Marc thought I was nothing more than a white man who *couldn't* think. How unfortunate it was that more white men and women weren't taking responsibility to eradicate school segregation—especially when it's so well known that school segregation is largely the result of segregated neighborhoods. How unfortunate it was that racial hatred was still so much a part of our lives in this country and how we as a people kept looking to others, or our government or institutions, to heal our raw nerve of race relations. How unfortunate it was that the only way I could be identified in this neighborhood was as a person in trouble or as a cop.

Why did I feel so alone? Why was I the only white teacher that I knew of who thought it made perfect sense to move into the predominately Latino and Black neighborhood of Watts where I worked. Didn't it make sense to anyone else that if we were going to heal all the racial hatred and make "equal" our segregated schools, that more and more people had to quit talking and writing about the problem and actually take individual responsibility and do something about it! Obviously, I was angry. But, then again, obviously as individuals, and as a society, we certainly had a long, long way to go.

Room for Rent

It was time to make a concerted effort to invite other teachers or social workers to move in with me in my house in Watts. I wanted to do something with all my anger and make a statement with my move, so why not establish a way that others could serve the community. If I were lucky, perhaps another idealistic young teacher would move in. For starters, I went to Teach For America in search of two young, idealistic teachers.

Teach For America (TFA) is a national teacher corps of talented, dedicated individuals from all academic majors and cultural backgrounds who commit a minimum of two years to teach in under-resourced urban and rural public schools. Typical corps members are young college graduates, looking to make a difference in education and children's lives. From what I knew of them, they were hard-working, motivated men and women. They would be a perfect fit for what I was hoping to accomplish in Watts.

When I gave the TFA headquarters in Los Angeles a call, the Program Director became interested in the idea immediately. She confessed that there had never been a TFA teacher who lived in the Watts community where they were teaching. Curious and supportive, she recognized the possibilities that could result from such an undertaking. We arranged to meet in her office later in the week.

When visiting with the Program Director, I explained that I was looking for TFA Los Angeles (TFA/LA) corps members who required more of themselves than the average teacher. I wanted individuals that had become involved with education in order to accomplish something significant. Basically, I wanted individuals such as myself to join with me as an equal in my move to Watts.

The Program Director encouraged me to write a short advertisement for their next newsletter, which would reach about three hundred corps members. With such a large number of individuals receiving the newsletter, the chances of getting someone to move in could be high. That night I went home, wrote the Teach For America invite and faxed it to her the next morning from school.

While I waited for the TFA/LA newsletter to be published, I spoke to Meghan about the idea. She was, afterall, a Teach For America teacher still in her first year of teaching. I tried to convince her to take one of the spare rooms, but she wasn't able to provide a definitive answer. Even with all of her visits—driving with me to look for a place to rent, looking over the house, coming over to work on our book—she was still considerably afraid of the area.

In my attempts to convince Meghan, I quickly became concerned that all TFA teachers would be too afraid to move into Watts, that they would not be far-sighted enough to realize the significance of my proposal. Obviously, I was becoming slightly discouraged.

4-H, for Sure!

The first day that Meghan received her TFA/LA Newsletter she brought it directly to my house. I was pleased to read my invitation to move into Watts in the Classified Section, but, by far, the best thing that I read was in the Resources For Educators section. It was there that Meghan discovered a grant possibility being offered by the Department of Housing and Urban Development. Apparently, the government agency was appropriating $3.5 million in funds for projects that develop 4-H afterschool programs for youths, ages seven to fourteen, in public housing communities.

Live in Watts

Hey, all you talented and dedicated Teach For America teachers interested in creating positive social change . . . listen up! I have a challenge for you. How would you *really* like to become an active participant in the under-resourced urban community in which you are teaching? Better yet, how would you like to move into Watts? Watts!?! Yes, Watts.

I'm inviting two of you to live with me, in a three-bedroom house located between the Hacienda Village and Nickerson Garden U.S. Department of Housing and Urban Development communities. Talk about getting involved! Remember your TFA Home, School, and Community Outcome Based Standards!?!

Our objective? To continue our participation as an equal member and beneficiary of the community in which we are working . . . to continue our involvement beyond the 9 to 5 professional working arrangement of which we are all too familiar. That's right, no more

continued on next page

darting out the door at the end of the day to go home to our comfortable, safe, living arrangements in Redondo Beach, Manhattan Beach, Hermosa Beach, or wherever you go to escape the inner city. You want to really make a difference? Then live in it!

What will we do? Well, you might find yourself enjoying some playful fun with some of your students without the pressure of actually having to teach them anything. Imagine that! You might find yourself riding to school on your bike and talking to a parent along the way. You might find yourself sitting down at a large round table in the middle of a dining room reading a book with one of your students. What a great mentorship possibility! You might find yourself becoming a friend with one of your student's parents. You might find yourself becoming involved with one of several community/social/educational organizations of which contact has already been initiated. You might find yourself contributing to the generation of knowledge that may be used in the future design of more inclusive, democratic learning communities. The possibilities are endless. It's up to you. Think of the many valuable experiences you'll acquire.

If you're interested in hearing more about this professional learning experience, give me a call at my new home.

Sincerely,

John Gust

P.S. Your rent will also be a heck of a lot lower than you're paying now!

Great! In spite of my efforts to change things, I knew that my work in the classroom would still be limited by conventional, standardized test-driven instruction as dictated by our administration and the greater Los Angeles Unified School District. And I also believed that the 4-H After School Activity Program at our school, at least in philosophy, nurtured the development of the whole child, with their "hands, head, heart, and health" approach. From all original appearances, the 4-H organization appeared to be the perfect organization for my class to team up with to implement the social action project we had in mind: The 4-H program was housed at our school, it had a community service component, and several children from my classroom were enrolled.

Ultimately, however, it would have been best for me to get out of the way so that the children in my classroom alone would've been able to complete every aspect of the project—from the negotiations onward. But the best I was able to do, given the realities of the situation and my inability to think otherwise, was to intercede and go with the 4-H organization, which was already allied with the Department of Housing and Urban Development.

I figured it would all work out, though. Meghan would be the architect and content expert who would teach all the kids how to design the playground, I would continue to be the process facilitator, and Compton Avenue Elementary School would be the educational agency that would sponsor the project. As Meghan and I began talking of the possibilities, we imagined how the playground area could be shaped just like a giant 4-H four leaf clover! Now all we had to do was convince 4-H that we had a great idea.

The first thing I did was to give the 4-H office in Los Angeles a call. I spoke to the Youth Development Advisor, and when I explained our idea she was very supportive. She suggested that I write a short proposal explaining the idea and then invited Meghan and I to attend a 4-H Vision Team meeting to give a brief presentation.

When we met with the Vision Team, which was sponsored primarily by Unocal, and explained our hopes, they were very supportive. However, at the meeting, we also discovered that the grants offered by the Department of Housing and Urban Development didn't directly affect Los Angeles and any new programs that might develop at the time. Fortunately, we did learn that the Housing Authority City of Los Angeles (HACLA), which managed the housing development, was soon to begin a $35 million rehabilitation and modernization project of the city's twenty-one public housing developments. This modernization project included a special emphasis on playgrounds! We also learned that HACLA was required to develop a submission package to be presented to HUD. This submission package was to be developed with the participation of, and in partnership with, the residents of the housing developments.

I knew many of the students at my school and in my classroom were residents of Hacienda Village, and I hoped that their input could be included. But I doubted that the bureaucrats involved would want to include children specifically in the design of the playgrounds. In spite of my original doubts, I vowed to continue my pursuits.

What Do You Guys Want to Learn About?

Remarkably, through use of the questions in the systems design methodology, we had been able to determine our main purposes, which at best had helped to provide a somewhat unclear focus for our efforts. And much to my surprise, our classroom's democratic struggles had produced a "happy" medium between that of total freedom and the resulting chaos on one end, and a type of participatory management on the other end. We were doing pretty much as

Angela had said we should do: Sometimes I made the major decisions, after getting input from the group, of course; sometimes the group voted on major issues, and the majority decided our direction; and at other times, consensual agreement was needed to determine our course. We had developed, and were following, our own ground rules. Enrolling my students in the rule-making process and their resulting struggles to become active members of the group significantly helped to organize our classroom. Overall, our emerging democracy wasn't as much of a battlefield as it was before. We were all getting along rather well.

Occasionally, the class required one of my "get real" talks. Generally, when I did this, I had to help them to remember that our site of struggle, whether we liked it or not, was still confined by the powerful constraints of the system that we were embedded within. Mostly, this helped my students to realize that it was very much a struggle for me, as the resource person, to arrange things the way they idealized—our Dream School was quite a bit harder to come to fruition than we had hoped.

In our "get real" talks I explained and tried to give reason to the kinds of things we all had to do in school. Things that were in many ways beyond my control. Things like standing and walking in straight lines, taking the standardized tests that were provided for us, our bell-regulated schedule, the loud yelling of the cafeteria workers during their lunch, and so on. I leveled with them, and shared all the things that the teachers had to battle, reason, and compromise with, too. I told them that I didn't like it either, that I had to do things that I didn't like or wasn't motivated to do, but reluctantly did because that was what was required. I told them about our meetings, the ton of paper work that I had to do, how I was mandated to teach certain things whether I liked it or not.

When I gave the class these occasional talks, I'd scan the room, noticing how they were all sitting so quietly in their seats. I'd see the looks on their faces. How depressed and sullen they were, as if they had just been delivered their oppressive fate. I watched their motivation, their spunk, their excitement about learning deteriorate. And I wished that there were something that I could do about it. Sometimes it seemed that our major purpose, our goal for what education was for, that of true happiness, would never come—our fight, our struggles would continue.

Finally, one day when I had just about all I could take of mandated curriculum and our administration's concern for rising scores on the next standardized milepost test, I decided to give my students another opportunity to voice their ideas on schooling. It was time to pose yet another series of questions employed by the systems design methodology I was using to develop our democratic classroom. This next series of questions would simply ask students what they most wanted to learn.

"You know what I'd like to do?" I asked. "I'd like to find out what all of you would like to learn about. I'm tired of everyone else telling us what we have to learn about."

"The first thing we need to do is to start thinking of questions. You can't just tell me, 'Mr. Gust, I want to learn about birds. Or Mr. Gust, I want to learn about the ocean.' You'll need to make questions out of the things that you want to learn about. And another thing . . . we'll need to organize our questions in some way, too. We need to think about what kinds of questions we have that will help us learn about ourselves, our community, and our world. That's how we'll group our questions."

"What do you guys think about that?" I asked.

"Yeah, that's a great idea, Mr. Gust," said Angela.

"Okay, then let me see your thumbs," I said. By now we were accustomed to raising our thumbs skyward if enthusiastic about a proposed idea, sideways if we were neutral, and downward if we didn't like the idea at all.

This time, every thumb pointed skyward. We had consensus, so I asked the paper monitors to pass out paper. Each person got three pieces of paper. On the first piece of paper, we each wrote the heading "What do you want to know about your self?" On the second piece of paper, we wrote the heading "What do you want to know about your community?" And on the third we wrote "What do you want to know about the world?"

Once we had our papers, I asked the class to write their questions on each of the three sheets. They could write as many questions as they could, but they had to write at least three. Right away, their little hands went to writing, and stayed that way for the next fifteen minutes.

That night I took home all their papers and compiled all of their questions into a file on my computer. Altogether, the kids generated a total of 109 different questions! There were questions that could've been grouped under all kinds of disciplines or fields of study. As a result of their questioning, we were going to have a classroom full of architects, astronomers, biologists, ecologists, geologists, meteorologists, sociologists, psychologists, physiologists, and urban designers. Together in our process of inquiry we were going to become anthropologists, cosmologists, metaphysicists, and theologians!

They posed astounding questions, questions that I couldn't wait to get started on: What makes the world go round? What is a community? How many muscles does Mr. Gust have? How is a baby born? Where do my ancestors come from? They asked wondrous questions: What is God? Where does God live? How does God die? I had no idea they wanted to learn such things! They wanted to know about how the sky was made, why their hair was so curly, how bugs fly, what made their brain tick, how they grew, why people die, where elephants came from, why people kept getting hurt, how much water was wasted in communities, and, very much like me and my current quest, who they were.

Boy, did I want to learn with these kids! As far as I was concerned we had just determined our curriculum for the entire year.

The following day, I brought in an enlarged, poster-sized computer printout of their questions. Together we decided to read through them all. When Danyell, the first to start, read Natasha's question, Natasha shouted out, "Hey, that's my question!" She was so proud.

While the kids continued taking turns reading all the questions, I couldn't help but to turn my attention to another poster, which our administration required teachers to have in clear sight on a wall in our rooms. It was a reminder of all our responsibilities. On it were listed all the basic skill objectives that we were mandated to explicitly teach our students to prepare them for the first of four standardized tests they were to receive that year.

What a difference in priorities! Here we were, busy reading some of the most profound, perplexing, and provocative questions of all time and I had to look over to that vacuous poster on my wall. The contrast was so ridiculous, it was funny. On it were nearly twenty basic-skill objectives, grouped according to three categories: language, reading, and mathematics. And the Lilliputian objectives were

Language

- Capitalizing beginning words in sentences and titles
- Identifying singular and plural nouns
- Knowing the difference between a question sentence and statement sentence
- Being able to determine the correct word order of a sentence
- Forming sentences by identifying the subject and predicate

Reading

- Identifying words that have the same beginning consonant blends (digraphs)
- Finding words that have the same medial long and short vowel sounds
- Identifying synonyms
- Being able to read a short story and identify that passage's details such as what, why, where, and when
- Analyzing a character in a story
- Making generalizations

Mathematics

- Add 2- and 3-digit whole numbers
- Subtract 2- and 3-digit whole numbers

- Numeration or identifying the one and tens place of a number
- Solving addition and subtraction word problems
- Identifying the geometric shapes of a triangle, circle, rectangle, and cylinder

As the kids took their turns reading the questions, I continued gazing at the poster, all the while wondering how I was going to fulfill my responsibilities while also addressing the deeper meanings behind the questions my students were providing. I wondered, did I even want to try? Did I just want to keep the poster up on the wall to satisfy the administration's requirements and close my door and go on about my day doing things the way my students and I wanted to? Or did I want to find a way to teach both the district's mandated basic-skill objectives while also addressing many of the larger issues that my student's questions raised? And which set of questions would drive my curriculum? Would the student's questions take priority, or would the district's objectives move into the foreground?

I wondered, if I followed these institutionalized objectives only in the way I was required, how many of my kids would become indifferent to new ideas? How many would lose their natural desire to learn because of the way they were required to experience learning? If they acquired these skills by means of automatic drill and practice, which was the accepted practice of the day, how many of them would lose their power of judgment and capacity to act intelligently in new situations? How many of them would come to identify the learning process with fatigue and boredom? How many of them would find that what they did learn was so foreign to the situations of life outside the school as to give them no power or control in their lives? How many would come to associate books with dull labor, so that they were conditioned to everything but the most flashy of reading material?

Their work needed to be driven by a purpose, their interests needed to be the primary determinant of the curriculum, and their work needed to be active and cooperative, not rote and drill. I was not going to force-feed them a long list of fragmented, atomized objectives so that they could darken in the little bubbles on yet another standardized test that assessed small bits of information that were totally out of any meaningful context.

In the end, I chose not to ignore the state-mandated curricular objectives, but I wasn't going to let them dictate my instructional practices either. The poster remained right where it was and the objectives continued to be my responsibility. Heck, I accepted those responsibilities when I took the job. They would just have to fit into and around the various tasks that would naturally arise in my classroom. And yes, I'd would teach those skills explicitly and thoroughly, meeting our mandated objectives, but now only through the process of "real" learning.

Sunday Morning in the 'Hood

Sunday was meant to be my first true "Community Day" in the neighborhood. I was prepared to spend the entire day being a full-fledged community member. I looked forward to the experience. Besides, it gave me an excuse to slow down, quit working for a while, and enjoy the passing time of day.

Earlier in the week, I asked Mr. Watkins about the church that he and his wife frequented. They went almost every Sunday to the 8:00 AM service at the Grant African Methodist Church on the corner of 104th and Central Avenue. I knew the church he was talking about. Oftentimes I would drive by the church on my way to the Bank of America ATM on the corner of 103rd and Central. It was fortunate to have the church within walking distance of my house. Mr. and Mrs. Watkins' daughter sang in the choir. And the old Reverend who had been with the church for a large number of years had recently passed, so the church had recently acquired a new reverend. According to Mr. Watkins, the current reverend was a young, energetic man who delivered very powerful messages. Mr. Watkins seemed pleased that the reverend always had something good and important to say on Sunday.

Meghan spent Saturday night on the couch at my house because she was interested in going to church the next day, and was beginning to get serious about renting one of the spare bedrooms. She stayed over to test things out before making a commitment. So on Sunday morning, Meghan and I woke up early to prepare for church.

While ironing my white shirt and suit pants, I somehow managed to, once again, short out the electricity in the house. The house's problems were only just beginning to emerge. Aggravated, I went outside to hit the breakers in the box and noticed Mr. Watkins across the street, wearing jeans. From the looks of it, Mr. Watkins wouldn't be going to church that morning. Dress at this Methodist church would definitely be formal. There would be none of the dressing down that could typically be found at many other churches in Southern California.

I finished my repair work at the breaker box, without saying anything to Mr. Watkins, and went back inside. Luckily, the electricity was functioning once again. I completed my ironing and got dressed. Meghan was ready, too. Rather than walk, we decided to drive the short distance to church. After Mass, we wanted to pick up some breakfast groceries and get a Sunday paper.

As soon as I got in the Jeep and began driving the short distance to church, I started feeling a little nervous. I didn't know exactly what to expect, and I certainly didn't know if the others would accept two white people into their church. Looking over at Meghan, I noticed that she was finally fully awake. As we rounded the corner and started on our way up Central Avenue, she instructed me to wake her up should she fall asleep during the sermon. I chuckled and told her that that would have to be her responsibility, not mine.

Once we made our way in and took our seats, it soon became apparent that there would be no falling asleep for either of us that morning. The Reverend Leslie White proclaimed and explained God's word in a very uplifting and demonstrative way. I wished that all sermons could be that way. As a fellow "teacher," I learned much from Reverend White that day. The choir was fantastic, too. I looked hard and long to find Mrs. Watkins' daughter Donna in the choir, but unfortunately she wasn't anywhere to be found.

I couldn't remember a time when I had had more fun in church. People were alive, emotional, and truly into worshipping the Lord in an energetic, uplifting way. I was truly moved. I cried. I laughed. And I was inspired to think deeply. You see, when I was growing up, I always felt that something was lacking in my church experiences. Going to church always felt like some type of social event with hollow rituals. Just like many teachers were now doing in their classrooms, the presider or priest read through some scripted material, and those in attendance, according to the script, responded, stood, sat, and kneeled right on cue. I don't ever remember experiencing church as a deeply spiritual experience.

According to the program booklet, which we were handed when we walked into the church, the theme of the day was "Creativity: To do always as much as we can, in the way we can, in order to leave our family, church, community, more beautiful and beneficial than we inherited it." How appropriate, how coincidental! I couldn't have picked a better day or better theme to complement my work at Compton Avenue School and in the Watts community.

Before the sermon, during the presentation of tithes and offerings, while kneeling at the altar, I made eye contact with Reverend White. Somehow, as the only white man in his church that day, I knew he would be looking at me. I also knew that his look would be serious in nature, but also very kind or cherubic as well. I looked up, pleased to see that, in fact, he was looking at me. We both smiled rather large smiles as a kind of acknowledgment and acceptance. After nodding, I bowed my head to say my prayers.

Normally, I wasn't in the habit of praying, at least not in the conventional way of kneeling down and reciting some memorized prayer. For me, praying was always more of a way of thinking, expecting, or visualizing God's will. And if my thoughts, expectations, visualizations, and desires were in alignment with the divine, well . . . .

However, as I somewhat skeptically began to pray that early morning in church, I remembered the billboard on the corner of Imperial Highway and Central Avenue that I would see whenever I got off the 105 Freeway to enter Watts. I passed by the billboard every morning on my way to work before moving into the neighborhood. It read, "Don't give up. Pray. It works." I often said out loud, doubtfully, as I passed by, "Yeah, right. Sure it does." But that day, because I was in Reverend White's church, because the day's theme of creativity coincidentally collaborated with my work in the neighborhood, I decided to give praying a try.

First, and selfishly, I prayed for my safety in the neighborhood. I was getting a little weary of being nervous and scared every time I walked or rode my bike through Hacienda Village on my way to work. Then I prayed for Mr. and Mrs. Watkins and their family. I wished them health and happiness. I prayed for Meghan, who provided so much encouragement and support. Gosh, she was working so very hard! In her first year of teaching, she was helping me to write a teacher resource book, getting involved with the possible playground project, and now thinking of moving into the neighborhood. I prayed that she would be safe, healthy, happy, and have an abundance of energy. Then I thought of the many children in my classroom. I could have prayed specifically for Donnell, or James, or Jobay, or Jennifer, or Angela, or Lakima, or any number of students that day, but I didn't. I prayed for them all. I saw something in my mind represented as "Youth." So I prayed for the youth of America that we so often seem to leave behind in our never-ending quest for economic growth and production.

Then I prayed for a little production and growth of my own. Perhaps the creation of something in Watts. Maybe the children's playground in Hacienda Village. Maybe it could become a physical reality rather than a visual image in my mind—God willing. Like the church program said, maybe I could leave *my* community, more beautiful and beneficial than I inherited it. I prayed, with everything I had, for all I was worth, to help make this dream come true. Involving myself and my students in a project that would provide an outlet for our creative drives would also provide a much-needed opportunity for nourishing our oftentimes neglected "spirits." Concluding my prayers, I said to myself, "Come on God, I gave praying a chance, help me make this playground happen!"

As Mass ended, everyone attending the service made their way out of church. Reverend White was standing at the door, giving hugs and handshakes to all that exited. As I hugged Reverend White, I thought about inviting him to my classroom so that he talk to my kids and explain what he did for a "living." But I decided to wait till later, after I gave it more thought. I didn't want to be hasty. Plus I wasn't sure that inviting a reverend into my public school classroom would be the appropriate thing to do. Besides, I think I was the one who had questions to ask, and my students probably wouldn't be interested. Mostly, I wanted to know how he, as a religious leader, involved himself with the surrounding community. I thought that I could probably learn a lot from Reverend White.

In the lobby, Meghan and I ran into Mrs. Watkins and her daughter Donna. It was a pleasure seeing their warm faces in church that morning. They were such good people. They made me feel so welcome in my new community. I told Donna that I was looking for her in the choir but wasn't able to find her. Mrs. Watkins explained that we were treated by a performance from the junior choir that day. "If that was the junior choir," I said, "the regular choir must be extraordinary!"

After saying good-bye, Meghan and I made our way out of the church lobby and walked to the Jeep in the parking lot. I quickly drove to the Food-4-Less to pick up a paper and some groceries for breakfast. I was starving. When we returned to the house, we made two large cheese, avocado, mushroom, and onion omelets, some hash browns, and toast. I loved making omelets on Sunday mornings.

Over breakfast, Meghan and I talked more about the possibility of her moving in. She was still undecided. In addition, it was also becoming painfully obvious that the Teach For America teachers were not going to respond to my advertisement. Perhaps, I reasoned, it had been too confrontational and challenging. I wished that I had been a little more tactful. If I had, then maybe Meghan and I wouldn't have been the only ones enjoying the omelets that peaceful Sunday morning in the 'hood.

Hangin' Out with My "Homies"

Hanging out was a very common thing to do in the 'hood. It was one of the community's strengths, I believe. Others might not have thought so, but I certainly did. Hanging out is good, hanging out is cool, hanging out is when people get together to talk, to laugh, to share, to just be. Unfortunately, it can also be a time to argue, fight, drink, sell and take drugs, and kill.

I did most of my hanging out on the front porch of my house. I felt a little safer there. A few boys from my class and the neighborhood got in the habit of coming by on their bikes with the goodies that they bought from the corner store. They'd eat their candy, cookies, and chips, talk, laugh, challenge each other, rough house, throw a ball around, and actually encourage one another. It was amazing to watch the social behavior of the boys at these times. It was markedly different from when they were at school.

For example, Donnell was a totally different kid when he was hangin' out with his "homies." Most of his friends told me that he was a very bad dude. And, when I considered his behavior when he wasn't in my classroom, I guess he was. In the room, he was one of my best behaved boys. He was polite, honest, trustworthy, generous, and hardworking. But man, when he was hangin' out, watch out, baby! Donnell's mouth carried the most bite. That dude could talk. And once he got going, there was no stopping him. He could out "dis" anybody—even me! When we were hanging out, to all the boys who came by the house, I was just one of their homies. Therefore, I wasn't treated any differently. Therefore, Donnell would rip me up!

While hangin' out on my porch, we would sometimes get ice cream from the ice cream truck that would often drive by. Before moving into Watts, the last time that could I remember getting ice cream from an ice cream truck was during my youth in Chicago. We'd hear the ice cream truck coming down the block and run out from wherever we were, while trying to pull out the small amount of change that we had from our pockets, or we would quickly run into the house to beg our mothers to give us some money. Now in Watts when the ice cream truck came around, the kids would jump all over me, begging for some change. If I had some, I'd give it to them. Heck, it was only fifty cents for an ice cream bar. Sometimes, though, I'd make them work for the money. There was always enough yard work to give them something to do.

Once in a while, instead of hanging around on my front porch, I would get out my bike and join the boys on a little romp through the neighborhood. I'd go with them wherever they wanted to go. Sometimes, I would speed up and challenge them to keep up with me. Once in awhile, we would head off towards Will Rogers Park, or just go around the block as fast as we could. People would look at us, or me, like I was crazy or something, but I didn't care; I was having a great time. My yearning for total joy and delectation was being satisfied through these simple, playful times.

Once, Lavell and his two friends Larry and M. H. came by on a Sunday afternoon. Larry and M. H. had bikes but Lavell didn't. I had an extra ten-speed with a flat tire that I never used, so I decided to give it to Lavell. He was pleased to get it. The three of them took off with their bikes and came back ten minutes later with the tires on Lavell's new bike inflated. They asked me if I wanted to take the Metro up to Franklin Delano Roosevelt Park Pool to go swimming for the day. I didn't have much to do, so I decided what the heck. The boys left their bikes in my living room, and I grabbed my swimming trunks, a towel, and some cash and took off. We walked to the Metro Station just past Compton Avenue School and got on. Minutes later, we were swimming.

Another time a kid that I had never met before came over with Donnell. He was a medium-sized boy named Valiant. I was interested in his name. I liked it a lot. I asked him if he knew what his name meant. Unfortunately, he didn't. I grabbed my dictionary from the end table in the living room and brought it outside. Then I sat down on the front steps with him and helped him look up his name. Once we found it, I had to read the definition to him because he still couldn't read. The definition jumped out at me. I made sure Valiant knew how important a name it was—"boldly courageous."

I loved those hanging-out times with the boys. The pressure was off; I didn't feel like I had to teach them anything in particular. I didn't have any pending test scores to worry about, no predetermined state-mandated curriculum to teach. This was a time for just the kids and me. And in many ways, in the process, I became their friend.

I had always found it curious how several experienced teachers and administrators that I had encountered over the years would say, "You can never be their friend. Being their teacher and their friend at the same time just doesn't work." I always felt they were wrong, but now I knew they were. And as far I was concerned, only when a teacher became a child's friend did the real learning start. Only then could any real "Lessons of Life" be learned.

Sometimes, the lessons were hard ones, such as when I had had enough of someone's foul mouth. I'd tackle him on the ground, roll him over on his back, and sit on his chest for a while. Then I'd tease him for a spell and eventually take a blade of grass and stick it up his nose. It would tickle him so much, he could barely stand it. Eventually, he'd pipe down, say "uncle," and promise to keep his mouth clean.

"Excuse Me . . ."

It was a Pupil-Free Day at Compton Avenue School. A great time for teachers to meet, compare notes, and prepare for instruction. Most of the teachers liked Pupil-Free Days. They were almost like vacation days. For some teachers, days went by much easier without kids around.

We had been meeting for about an hour and a half when Mrs. Ruiz allowed all of us to take a ten-minute break. I wanted to get some air, so I went outside. I walked over to the parking lot in back of the school so I could get a book out of my Jeep. I figured I could get in some light reading before heading back into the meeting.

Ms. Rosenberg, a fourth-grade teacher, must have had a similar idea when she followed me out to the parking lot. Actually, she wanted to grab a quick cigarette. I was hoping to be able to have some quiet time by myself, but it looked like the opportunity wouldn't present itself. Ms. Rosenberg wanted to talk while she smoked. A new law prevented teachers from smoking on school grounds at any time, so in order to comply with the law, Ms. Rosenberg motioned for me to walk with her over to the fence that bordered our school. She probably figured that the fence would be close enough to being off school grounds—besides, no one would see us there anyway. I brought my book with me, doubting that I'd get a chance to do any reading.

Ms. Rosenberg opened up a conversation about a book that I had lent her several weeks ago. I began to wonder if I were ever going to get it back. When we finished talking about the book, Ms. Rosenberg, never one to be short of something to talk about, told me about some socially proactive and intellectual friends that were visiting her from her country of origin, Ethiopia. She wanted me to meet them. Explaining that I looked forward to the opportunity, two large groups of people in Hacienda Village on the other side of the fence starting walking our way. They looked out of place because they were wearing suits and uniforms—police uniforms. I wondered what they were doing there.

Ms. Rosenberg whispered, "They're probably here because of that person who was killed there recently."

With a puzzled look on my face I said, "I didn't know somebody was killed there."

"You didn't know that?" she asked. "Yeah, just last week someone was shot right around there."

Getting nosier by the second, I asked, "Do you think we should try to find out what they were doing?"

Without answering, Ms. Rosenberg called out to the first group, "What are you doing?"

It was apparent that the first group of people weren't going to respond to Ms. Rosenberg's inquiry. It was probably the way she approached them. Actually, she didn't approach them at all; rather, she just yelled out to them as they were passing by.

Still feeling nosy about who they were and what they were doing, I walked up close to the fence and said, "Excuse me, I'm a teacher here at Compton Avenue School and I also live in the neighborhood, on 107th Street. It may be none of my business, but since I'm a little nosy and, after all, this is now my neighborhood, too, may I ask what you're doing here today?"

One of the policeman responded right away. He explained that they were doing something about the security in the area. Then the group introduced themselves. Don J. Smith, the Executive Director, and Milton Patterson, the Director of Resident Relations of the Housing Authority, introduced themselves first. Hubert Taylor, the manager of Hacienda Village, introduced himself next. Finally, the two uniformed officers from the Los Angeles Police Department, Senior Lead Officer Michael Lockett of the Southeast Division and his supervisor, Sergeant Ted Maillet, the Senior Lead Coordinator of the Southeast Division, introduced themselves.

I couldn't believe it. What a wonderful coincidence! Here I was still trying to figure out how to make the pending playground project become a reality, and now I was getting a rare chance to meet some major "players" from the Housing Authority.

"Well," I said, "I'd offered to shake your hands, but I think that would be a little difficult to do through the fence."

As Ms. Rosenberg listened, I explained my recent field trip through Hacienda Village and the posting of our posters. I also mentioned how I was trying to start an after-school project involving the 4-H club in an effort to redesign the run-down park that was at the western-most end of Hacienda Village.

Milton Patterson then spoke up and explained that he was on the 4-H Vision Team. I couldn't believe my ears; not only was I was talking with people from the Housing Authority, but now I was making contact with yet another official on the Vision Team. I couldn't have arranged this coincidental phenomenon in a million years. I told Mr. Patterson that I would probably be attending the next Vision Team meeting to continue the discussion about our playground renovation idea.

Needing to get back to continue our morning's meeting, I thanked the gentlemen for their time, promised that they would be hearing from me, and walked with Ms. Rosenberg back to my Jeep to drop off my book before going back into the school.

Excited by the coincidental meeting during our morning break, I barely paid attention to anything that was discussed for the remainder of the morning. At lunch time, I darted out the door and jumped in my Jeep and sped away to the Nickerson Gardens Administrative Offices. I wanted to get a map of Hacienda Village so that I could explain where the children's park was located. Once I reached the Nickerson Garden's parking lot, I parked the Jeep and hurriedly walked into the office. There was a large portrait of the Executive Director, Don J. Smith, on the wall directly behind the receptionist.

Unfortunately, the receptionist didn't have a map of Hacienda Village to give to me, but she was able to direct me to the Avalon Gardens, Administrative Offices on the corner of 88th and Avalon. My lunch time was quickly running out, so I ran back to my Jeep and drove off as fast as I could. When I arrived at Avalon Gardens I realized that the minor inconvenience was actually a blessing in disguise, because who should be standing there but Hubert Taylor, the manager of the Hacienda Village. As I approached the front desk, Mr. Taylor offered his hand for me to shake.

"I didn't want to waste any time after our chance meeting, so here I am." I said.

Hubert smiled warmly and invited me into his office. We began a brief chat about my hopes for the children and the playground. As I explained the idea further, he seemed genuinely interested and enthusiastic. I asked him if it were all possible to receive funding for the project, and he had to confess that he didn't really know the answer. However, he was able to give me the name and the number of the person who would be able to give me more information about the planned future development of the playground area. His name was Sanford Riggs, the Construction Grounds Supervisor. Mostly, I wanted to know if the prior plans or design for the renovation of the playground area were etched in stone, because if they weren't, I had a great idea about how we could involve the kids in the design of *their* playground.

Finished with our discussion, I bid Hubert farewell, exited the building with the map, and climbed back in my Jeep. All I had originally hoped for from my pursuits that afternoon was a map of Hacienda Village, so this was a very productive trip. When I started my Jeep, I realized not only that I was running late, but also that I was extremely hungry. In the rush to get the map, I hadn't stopped to eat. I decided to duck into the McDonald's drive-through on the corner of 103rd and Avalon. Swallowing the last bite of my Big Mac, I turned the Jeep into my school's parking lot.

Grabbing my coke and French fries, I ran into the main building and entered the meeting, which was already in progress. I was late, but nobody seemed to notice. When the day-long meeting finally concluded, I decided to share all my newly acquired information with Mrs. Ruiz. She was genuinely excited and expressed her interest in participating or contributing to my quest.

With all the coincidences and the apparent support from Mrs. Ruiz, I went home feeling very optimistic. Perhaps all of my prayers were going to be answered. Now all I had to do was build up enough strength to deal with the combined bureaucracies of LAUSD, HACLA and 4-H.

Are Our Scissors Sharp Enough?

In the notice that went out to the residents of Hacienda Village, which I picked up from Hubert Taylor at the Avalon Administrative Offices, I discovered that a meeting was soon to take place that would enable residents to participate meaningfully in the planning and implementation of the modernization project that was to effect all of the Housing Authority's housing developments. The notice stated that residents would have an opportunity to help identify priority projects for modernization, and provide community consensus and feedback about the implementation of the projects.

Even though we weren't residents of the housing community, Meghan and I went to the meeting to see what it was all about, to watch how consultants and officials from HACLA communicated with residents, and to see if we could convince them to allow the children to become involved in the design of our targeted playground. In hindsight, I wished I had brought my students along to the meeting. It would have been a good experience for them.

At the meeting, we listened as it was explained that the money would be used to beef up security by installing more bars on doors and windows, to erect a tall fence around the community, to provide bulletproof lights, and, finally, to start a community crime prevention group. We watched the nonparticipatory, outside consultants make a feeble attempt to gather input from the ten or so residents present from a community of approximately 200 residents. One very loud, angry man stood up to ask that the boards covering up his windows be replaced with glass. Very little was contributed by the other residents. As we watched the consultants fulfill their obligation and leave, I couldn't help but wonder if they went home thinking, like so many often do, that the residents wouldn't or couldn't generate very much input. I wondered if they considered, even for a brief second, that their techniques of facilitating productive dialogue were ineffective. Certainly, in my opinion, there was no "meaningful participation" occurring on that day.

When the meeting was over, we were able to hand our proposal to HACLA's Construction Support Supervisor, Sanford Riggs. We also met the President of the Residents' Association, Richard Linzey. He lived in Hacienda Village, and because we were actually becoming advocates for the residents, he was very supportive. I went away from the meeting feeling positive about the possibilities, but also outraged about what I believed was the injustice of inadequately gathered input by the consultants.

A few days later I called Sanford Riggs to ask him about the proposal. He told me that he hadn't had the time to look it over yet. But I saw him reading it outside after Meghan and I had given it to him! We were both talking to a resident about my students hopes and plans for the playground and he was taking a long time to read it over. I know because I watched him out of the corner of my eye the whole time we were talking to the older lady.

In our telephone conversation, he said that he was going to show it to his boss. A good bureaucratic buck-passing opportunity if I ever saw one. He also mentioned all the possible legal and liability restraints. This *was* something that I neglected to consider, but did he have to keep putting more red tape in our way?

When I got off the phone with him, my negative thinking started getting the best of me again. I kept thinking to myself that this community playground area was never going to happen. Nobody would want to allow the children and community members to be a part of this. Oh, the Housing Authority would, of course, testify that they wanted to involve the residents in any modernization changes that they were going to make; they would garner the residents input, write their report, submit it to the proper authorities, and hire on fifty-one percent of the crew from the housing projects to help in the manual labor of making the changes, but would it make a significant and real difference? Would it adequately and effectively gather substantial input from the residents? Would they make the extra effort to really get people involved? Doubtful.

After a depressing week of negative thinking, Sanford Riggs called me! Was I surprised! We made arrangements for Meghan and me to meet with him and his boss, the Assistant Director of Housing Maintenance. Feeling optimistic, we went to their construction offices thinking that we were actually making progress. But when we got there, they said that while they liked our idea, the time was too late; the playground's plans had already been drawn up, there wasn't enough money, and so on, and so on. I was pissed! Sanford called me up and made arrangements for us to meet him and his boss so that they could tell us that? When that meeting was over, I vowed to quit all my feeling sorry for myself and to play the game, so I could find some way to cut through all the red tape.

It became obvious quickly that we were going to need a very large, sharp pair of scissors. There was a lot of red tape in our path. And maybe what we really needed was something a little more effective than a pair of scissors!

How Do You Want to Learn All This Stuff?

So, we had our general ground rules established, we had already decided on our main purposes—happiness, to help others, and simply to learn, for learning's sake—and we had determined the multitude of things that we wanted to learn. Now, in our systems design process, all we needed to do was to figure out how we were going to learn all that stuff.

By identifying how we wanted to learn, we were also making sure that our day-to-day living was also consistent with our mission. Happiness, compassion, and learning weren't just supposed to be an end result, something that arrived after we learned what we learned, but rather something that emanated from everything we did. We had to describe how we in our classroom wanted to learn on a day-to-day basis while in pursuit of our vision.

"Okay, you guys," I started. "We know now what all of you want to learn. All of your questions on this poster I made tell us that. Now what we need to do is to figure out how we're going to learn those things."

"So, for me, the first thing I need to know is how I should be teaching. I need to know what kinds of things I should be doing as your teacher. I'll write the question on the board, and you give me your answers."

"Okay, so here's the question." Quickly, I wrote, How will your teacher teach in your classroom? on the board and then circled it. "All right, start thinking and give me your answers." As they did, as usual, I clustered their responses on the board.

- Ask students what they want to learn, and then if the teacher knows what the student wants to learn, then they can help them.
- The teacher should bring a lot of cool stuff to school, show us that stuff, and then we get to decide what we get to do.
- The teacher can bring in lots of books for us to read.

Surprisingly, they were all satisfied with just those three responses. Originally, I thought that maybe they were just tired that day, or didn't much feel like doing anything at all. But then I figured that I was just asking the question the wrong way. So, I rephrased the question in hopes of eliciting additional responses.

"Okay, that's pretty good. It gives me an idea of what you're expecting from me. It sort of makes me feel like a resource person. You know, I bring in stuff, books and things, and we decide what to do with them. Now what I think I need to know is how it will look in here when we are all using the stuff, the books and things, that I'll be bringing in. In other words, what is it going to look like in here, what are we all going to be doing, when we're learning all those things that you've already decided upon."

To gather their responses, of course, on the board I wrote the following question: What kind of learning experiences will you have? But this time, they seemed to be having some difficulty. Blank faces filled the room. I don't know if it was because they didn't know how to answer the question—obviously, they had no prior knowledge of equity pedagogy, teaching to student strengths, learning styles, modalities, domains, or all those other ways we design the learning experience to meet student needs—or if they were just disinterested. Maybe by this time they didn't care how they would learn. Thankfully, I chose the former.

"Okay," I said. "It looks like you guys are having a difficult time with this, so I think I'm going to help." They didn't seem to mind, so I kept going. "As I said, what I want to know is what it's going to look like in here when we're all learning. What's it going to look like, be like, in here so that we are happy, helping others, and learning. You know, just like you said when we talked about what our school was for. Let me give you some examples. Am I always going to be up at the chalkboard talking to all of you, or will you be working together in groups trying to learn or do something, or will each of you be working by yourselves, like researching something, or will each of you be taking turns once in awhile to teach the others?"

That's when the hands shot up. Now they got it! It seemed that everyone had an opinion. Without being called on, Angela started us off. "Why don't we do all of those things?"

Angela always put a huge grin on my face. "You know, Angela, that's what I thought, too. I agree. But let's get everybody's answers down, too." Wanting to use their own language, I clustered their answers on the board.

- We can have small groups to read so that they can help each other.
- Sometimes you (the teacher) can tell all of us things that we want to know.

- Each of us can work alone to learn something, sometimes, if we want.
- Kids have to do or make something that other students can use to learn from.

Once again, they were satisfied with just those few answers. And that was okay. I guess, from all I could think of, they seemed to cover all the bases. Now all we had to do was to get busy.

Shootin' Hoops

Just like he said he would, Victor arrived at school exactly at 2:30 when the kids were getting out. He was smiling his usual big ear-to-ear smile. When Victor smiled, his big cheeks would swell up like a muscle does when it contracts. His smile was contagious. Victor was always good to see; he had a certain way about him that made you happy and proud to be who you were.

I drove my Jeep to school that day in order to run some errands in the morning before school started, so I had to drive home to change clothes. I also wanted to go home to get something quick to eat and pick up my new basketball. I knew I would need the extra fuel, plus I didn't want him to think that I was a novice basketball player without the proper equipment. Danyell asked if she could come with me, so she and I walked to my Jeep in the parking lot as Victor walked across the street to the basketball court in Hacienda Village. His plan was to round up some players before I got there. I quickly drove the three blocks home, with Danyell securely seat-belted in the front seat.

When we arrived at the house, I let Danyell turn on the television while I went into my bedroom, closed the door, and quickly changed into my new basketball clothes. Once I was finished getting dressed, I washed all the crud off my face from the day. You won't believe how much chalk tends to settle there from a full day in the classroom. After I was finished getting freshened up, Danyell and I had a 7-Up. Then I grabbed my brand new, sparkling clean basketball, and we began walking down to the Hacienda Village basketball court.

As Danyell and I took turns bouncing the basketball back and forth, I asked, "So Danyell, who do you think's going to win?"

"Whatever team my daddy's on," she answered matter of factly.

"Well, then," I said stealing the ball away from her, "I'll just have to make sure I'm on your daddy's team."

When we got to the court, Victor was already playing a game with two of his homies. He was playing alone against the two of them—and he was winning. He was hot and he knew it. He kept making every outside shot like it was nothing. And to make it even worse, he kept taunting his competitors, "Watch this one now. It's goin' down. Oh, baby, I'm hot. I can't miss. Watch it.

Watch it, now." Victor owned the court. Watching him, I realized Danyell was right. I had to be on his team.

I was a little anxious that day, but it probably wasn't any different than how I would feel entering any new social situation. But, I must admit, playing basketball with a bunch of guys from the ghetto, in a housing development, was a "slightly" different situation for me altogether. Or so I thought.

While waiting for Victor to finish his game, I shot baskets for awhile with little Marvin. Marvin went to school at Markham Jr. High. Markham was right across the street from Compton Avenue Elementary School and the Hacienda Village basketball court. For some time, Marvin had been coming around the house to check me out and to hang out. Most of the time, he had nothing else better to do. I liked Marvin, but he wasn't much good at basketball. He didn't care, though; he just wanted to shoot some hoop like the rest of us.

Our game started after Victor demolished his two opponents by a landslide. When I walked onto the court, I nervously introduced myself to the two other players. One of the guys gave me a warm look, smiled, and said, "God Bless."

"Thank you," I said, somewhat surprised by his sincerity. I guess I didn't know what to expect, but I certainly didn't think I'd be accepted this readily.

Victor told the other two guys that he and I would be on the same team. I thought it was very gracious of him. "Victor, you know, I don't think you know what you're gettin' into. Now you're going to be playing with a handicap."

"How do you figure? What's my handicap?" Victor asked.

"Me!" I answered.

Gracious guy that he was, Victor responded, "Naw!"

As we started to play, I made an effort to keep my eyes on the sidelines. I wanted to see what kind of reaction my playing there would create. Were the residents going to be offended by my presence? Would they be amazed? Would they be suspicious? As far as I knew, anything could happen. I kept thinking that someone was going to walk up to me and ask what I was doing on their turf. I half expected someone to try and pick a fight with me.

One thing I did know, though, was that Victor would stand up for me and confront anyone who tried to give me a hard time. Actually, I felt well protected by Victor. From all his stories and his reputation, I knew he could hold his own against any possible trouble that might develop.

Opposite of all my fears, the neighborhood began to trickle out to watch us play. All kinds of kids from Hacienda Village and school showed up. Most of the kids I knew, and a few I didn't. A few older Black guys showed up, too. The looks they gave were a little suspicious, but nothing out of the ordinary, considering the circumstances. They might have thought that I was a cop or something, but I really think that they didn't much care one way or the other.

During the game, Victor had enough energy to keep score for all of us. On the other hand, I was doing my best just to stay alive. I was dying out there! At one point during the game, Victor and I were down by a few points, but then I got my second wind. I didn't want to look like a wimp, so I rallied my strength, thought about the significance of the game, and put on my competitive nature. We came from behind to finally win the game. I scored four baskets. Victor scored the rest. I surprised myself, but was happy when the game was over.

I practically died. After shaking the other guys hands, and giving Victor a couple of high fives, I laid down—or rather collapsed—on the ground next to the bench where a group of older men had been sitting watching the game. I was sweating, huffing and puffing so bad that Victor came over, with his wide, now-taunting smile, to see how I was doing.

"John, John, are you okay, John?"

"Get out of here!" I yelled. "I'm all right. Just a little tired is all."

The old guys on the bench murmured and laughed under their breath a bit. They were obviously amused. I took about ten minutes to revive myself, but not Victor. He kept smiling and shooting baskets while continuing to rub our victory in the other players' faces.

A few minutes later, Victor was ready to get another game going. He came over to the bench where I was now sitting, still sweating and talking with one of the guys. He asked, "You want to get in on the next game?" Still trying to catch my breath from the first game, I politely declined. Victor looked at me and smiled. "What's wrong, John? You're not tired, are ya?" "Of course I'm tired. What the hell does it look like?" I yelled back. We all laughed while Victor turned away to finish pulling together his next game.

All I wanted to do was to sit there, let the sweat pour off my body, and talk with the guys. One of the guys was entirely shocked to discover that I had recently moved into the neighborhood. Like many of his peers, he had recently taken flight from the ghetto and was now living in Riverside, a primarily white, suburban neighborhood. Together we noted the contrast between our decisions and realized how interesting it all was.

After Victor finished up his *fourth* game, he joined those of us still sitting on the bench talking. The religious fellow—the one who said "God Bless" at the beginning of the game—also joined the conversation. When he sat down next to me, he began to explain how he read and studied the Bible every day.

Victor, playing with him a little, asked, "Hey man, do you really believe in God?"

Not too pleased with Victor's teasing at this point, he wouldn't answer. Instead, he shook his head and looked the other way.

"What about you, John, do you believe in God?" asked Victor.

Not entirely sure if Victor were still playing, and somewhat reluctant to start a full-fledged conversation concerning my thoughts and feelings about God, I gave Victor my short answer. "Yeah, I do, Vic."

I was somewhat surprised that the guys there seemed willing to talk about God. I couldn't ever remember talking about God with any of my other friends—ever. It just wasn't something that was discussed. It was always one of those topics that everyone attempted to avoid. Too risky, too consuming, too . . . difficult to talk about. I disliked that, too. I always was one to become bored when conversations remained centered on trivial, unimportant things. You know, stuff like football games, cars, the price of food in the supermarket, television shows, people's vacations, traffic in Los Angeles, you name it. I'd sit there listening, or, more accurately, trying to listen, wondering why. Why did life always have to be so mundane? Was it because people were always so afraid to talk about more meaningful things? Or was it because they simply had no interest in those things? I always wondered that. Then I'd try to fit in, try to participate, try to become involved, but always found myself becoming so bored, so quickly. I'd sit there hoping, waiting for someone to turn the conversation into something a little more meaningful. Then, on those rare occasions when the talk would turn that way, I'd usually perk up and get too intense about it. I'd leap into it like a starved person diving into a big, juicy steak. Clawing, slobbering, chomping away. Unfortunately, most people would find that too overwhelming and then quickly shy away from any further talk on the "meaningful" issue.

So, knowing how things usually got when I ran into a conversation like that, I desired to cool it down before someone else shied away from the topic. I jumped up off the bench, slapped Victor on the back, and said, "Well, big fella, its about time for me to get heading back home."

Right away, Victor offered to walk me home. I tried to explain that I'd be all right, but he still wanted to make sure I wouldn't run into any trouble. Victor was as cognizant as I was of what the neighborhood was like. Mostly though, he wanted me to be seen with him so all of the locals would be a little more comfortable with my presence. I didn't complain, because Danyell and Brianna, Victor's younger daughter, joined us on our walk home as well.

As we made our way through some of the busier sections of Hacienda Village, with Brianna holding onto my hand, Victor made a point of saying hello and waving to everyone he knew—which seemed like everybody living there. He was certainly doing a good job of introducing me to the neighborhood. We made it out of Hacienda Village and then walked the short distance down 107th Street towards my house.

When we got to my house, I unlocked the four locks on the two front doors and invited everyone in. Danyell remarked how nice the house was. I was amazed at the difference between my perspective and that of Danyell's. The house was still much in need of repair.

I told Victor the story of my stolen VCR and who I thought stole it. He knew Pee Wee, and I got the impression that he didn't much like him either. From the way it sounded, he and Pee Wee had probably had a few tussles in the past. With a quick smile, Victor sort of let me know who won those conflicts, too. Then he told me not to worry about my VCR, he would get another one for me. I didn't ask any questions.

After standing around inside the living room area talking for those first few minutes, I unlocked the large lock on my bedroom door. Right away, Danyell ran into the room and jumped on my bed. I reacted and raised my voice, telling her to get off. I had a nice clean, cream-colored duvet and comforter, and I certainly didn't want a dirty little kid messing it up.

But then, thinking that I had been a little too harsh, I said, "Sorry Vic, I didn't mean to yell. I just didn't want her getting my bed dirty."

Victor reassured me, "It's all right with me, John. You can yell at her whenever you want. It's your bed."

Once I was finished giving Victor, Danyell, and Brianna the introductory tour of the house, we sat down with cold sodas in the living room to continue our conversation. We talked about exercise and getting in shape. I had a lot of work to do in order to get into the kind of shape Victor was in—heck, I was still wheezing from our basketball game! Victor knew about my body-building career and he started to ask about it again. To prove to Victor that I wasn't just throwing him a line, I pulled out from under the coffee table an old photograph album with pictures from my body-building days. He looked at the pictures while I got another soda for Danyell and Brianna.

Victor was impressed with the photos. He was as interested in strength and muscles as were most of the younger boys that came over to the house. It surprised me that others were still impressed by my body-building days because it had ceased to impress me for quite some time. Funny how things change. What impressed me the most about people was their intellect, not their muscles. But not Victor, he said that, more than anything, he wanted to look the way I once did.

Considering Victor's build and shape, I told him that it was certainly possible. "What we need to do is take you to the gym and get you started working out—proper like."

"Do you think you could write me up a training routine and diet schedule?" he asked.

With all that Victor had done for me, that was the least I could do. "Yeah, that'll be easy."

While the girls played with the toys and read the books that I had on the shelf in the dining room, Victor and I continued talking. We got on the subject of Compton Avenue Elementary School before too long. I found out that

Victor once worked there as a campus aid for a few years. He knew pretty much everything there was to know about all the gossip and the goings on at the school. He also went there when he was a kid. We talked about the neighborhood, a fight he recently had, my old days working as a bouncer at a few bars in Chicago, his being married, my still being single.

We also talked about Danyell and her behavior and progress in the classroom. With Danyell listening closely, I explained to Victor how I saw Danyell as a chameleon of sorts. She always seemed to be changing colors, so to speak, in order to be just like the people she was sitting next to or interested in becoming friends with. To me, Danyell's behavior, which was occasionally flavored with what we teachers call "attitude," was typically dependent on how she thought she should act in order to be accepted by others. It amazed me how much the need for peer group conformity was dictating her behavior. I got the impression, and Danyell said so herself, that she didn't much like herself. At that point, Victor explained to me that she was doing it for the attention. I wasn't convinced entirely, but decided to take his word for it for the time being. He was, after all, Danyell's father.

Brianna was still playing with the toys on the rug, but by now, because of her interest in our conversation, Danyell had worked her way over to the coffee table. Right there in front of her, Victor gave me permission to hit Danyell: "John, anytime she gets out of line in the room, anytime she gets one of her attitudes, just like I told Ms. Johnson when Danyell was in the first grade, I want you to hit her. I want you to take her out in the hallway and smack her behind. And do it good, too. Don't hold anything back."

Not knowing what to do, I looked over at Danyell and noticed that she was smiling. She seemed to like the idea! It was almost as though this hitting thing was, in Danyell's mind, an expression of love or care. Hitting her meant that you cared about her?

I wasn't as convinced. Personally, I couldn't imagine myself hitting a child. Oh, at times I've wanted to and imagined what it would be like to physically lash out at a child. But I could never bring myself to do it! Looking for a way out, I told Victor, "Yeah, but, Vic, that's against the law now you know. I could get fired for doing that."

Victor looked at me and strongly said, "If anyone gives you a hard time about it. You just tell them to come see me!"

I told him, "I don't know, Vic, I just can't see myself hitting a child. That's just not my way. I don't know if I could do it. I have a hard enough time handing out punishments or reprimands in class as it is. As for hitting a child, that's another thing altogether. I don't know, man."

From the looks of it Victor and Danyell knew I meant it, too. I hoped I didn't disappoint them.

It was getting late and we were all pretty tired—at least I was—so our conversation finally came to an end. As we said our good-byes and I walked my guests out the door, Danyell asked, "Mr. Gust, do you think I could stay overnight at your house sometime?"

"We'll see, Danyell," I offered. "It depends on what your mother and father say."

I really didn't want her sleeping over at all. I didn't want to have to deal with anyone knowing that I had a female student spending the night with me. I didn't think it would be too smart, especially after Danyell's eagerness to lie down on my bed. A young female student spending the night with a single male teacher? Other colleagues had already commented on how I was transgressing the traditional student–teacher relationship by inviting students into my home.

As I stood on my front porch, watching Victor walk down the sidewalk with his two daughters, back towards Hacienda Village, thoughts about the schoolday and my activity in the neighborhood filled my head. It was definitely a full day. It was Career Day at school, so I had the opportunity to meet several actors, I dined with a few firefighters at lunch, I played basketball with Victor and the guys, and visited with Victor, Danyell, and Brianna at my home. I thought about how "rich" I was, how fortunate, how lucky. Everybody told me that I was crazy for moving into Watts, but as far as I was concerned, they were unfortunate not to have an opportunity such as this. For once, I was happy to be a teacher living within a couple of blocks of the school at which I taught, in Watts. My friend Marc was wrong, this white man *could* think.

Powerful Petition

After playing phone tag with Sanford Riggs from the Housing Authority for several weeks, another meeting was arranged. Apparently, the Housing Authority was still willing to listen to our ideas. I was excited about the possibilities, but this time I wanted to be prepared. To demonstrate our commitment, I planned to gather the support of the residents of Hacienda Village with a petition. What I really wanted to do was to plop the petition, with two hundred signatures, down in front of HACLA officials and watch to see how they would respond.

The meeting arranged with HACLA wasn't for another week, so there was still time to write a petition and gather signatures. The first thing to do was to call Richard Linsey, the President of the Residents Association, while on my lunch break at school. Richard lived in Hacienda Village, so he knew the people living there rather well. On the phone, Richard and I agreed to meet at the Hacienda Village Social Hall the next day after school. Satisfied that we were beginning to make some progress, when I went home, I called Meghan and asked her to join me for the meeting.

When Meghan and I arrived for the meeting the next day, Richard and his secretary, Tamika, greeted us at the door. The meeting was a good one. Richard was very supportive and appreciative of our efforts. Tamika, a long-time resident of Hacienda Village and a student at Compton College, thought that the petition would be a good tactic for trying to persuade the Housing Authority to take on the project. When I asked her if she were willing to help us gather signatures, she volunteered enthusiastically.

It was decided that, because of our time constraints, I would write up the petition, and in two days we would get together to take it around to the residents in Hacienda Village. As much as I would've liked to involve my students and residents from the housing development in this whole process, I reluctantly wrote the petition the next day. Obviously, the combined aspects of the reality of our situation and my obsessive orientation towards the completion of a task took away from the ideal way this student-generated social action project should have proceeded.

Once Meghan translated the petition into Spanish, I faxed it over to Deirdre Thompson from the 4-H organization. We wanted her, and 4-H, to be aware of our efforts.

In the petition, our first objective was to inform the residents about the problem:

> The children and residents of Hacienda Village have not been given the opportunity to become "adequately" involved in HACLA's current rehabilitation and modernization project as it applies specifically to the upgrade of the playgrounds and tot lots in Hacienda Village.

After the residents were aware of the problem, our second objective was to explain exactly what we wanted to do about the problem:

> We want the children and residents of Hacienda Village to be given much more of an opportunity to be actively and adequately involved in HACLA's modernization project. We want the children and residents to participate in more meaningful activities in regards to the planning and completion of the upgrade of the playgrounds in Hacienda Village. We want to involve the children enrolled in the 4-H After-School Program at Compton Avenue Elementary School in a community service project to help accomplish this task. These 4-H participants are some of the children that play in these playground areas. We believe that by enrolling these "community members" in this project, as they work with other Hacienda Village residents, it will help to meet the needs of the community and children while promoting a sense

of ownership, thus building a greater sense of responsibility for future upkeep and maintenance of the areas.

So with completed petitions all ready and in hand, on Friday after school, Tamika, Meghan, a few of the young teens hanging out in the area, and I set off to get as many signatures as possible. Just then, Victor pulled up in his car. That afternoon, he was in the neighborhood visiting with some of his old friends. Naturally, I had to ask him if he wanted to help. And naturally, because of his generous ways, Victor said, "If it's for the kids . . . sure, no problem." That afternoon, our team acquired more than 130 signatures! A good number, but not good enough.

By Sunday, I was ready to go out to get some more signatures. While canvassing the housing development, I first encountered a jovial group of ladies sitting outside on their front porch, drinking a few beers. They were laughing and having a great time. It was a hot day and I would've loved a beer, but, unfortunately, they didn't offer.

After getting their signatures, I next met a woman sitting by her back door having dinner. When she found out what I was doing, she practically ripped the clipboard out of my hand, saying, "Give me that petition. It's about time somebody did something around here for the kids." After she finished signing, she invited me to join her for dinner. She was having ox tails and greens.

"My mother used to make ox-tail soup when I was younger," I said. "I loved it." And I was getting kind of hungry, too, but many signatures were still needed. Hoping not to offend her, I politely declined and went on my way.

A few minutes later, I encountered a man who answered the door, holding a very large switchblade in his right hand. Apparently, he didn't want any trouble. Once he discovered what I was doing, however, he folded the knife, put it back in his pocket, and signed the petition.

That afternoon, we reached our mark. We picked up an additional seventy-four signatures. We had reached our goal of 200!

By the middle of the next week, we had our meeting with people from the Housing Authority. Earlier that day, during school, I took my class on a field trip to the L. A. Zoo. We had a fabulous time watching the monkeys eat their own excrement (the kids enjoyed that the most; you should have seen them laugh), watching the big gorilla pound his chest, and watching the big Indian python slither along in its glass cage. The kids were a ton of fun, but a lot to handle. Actually, they were much easier to "handle" than I had originally anticipated, simply because Danyell's father, Victor, came along.

Victor could be an extremely formidable presence when he wanted to be. He could be downright scary. He really kept the kids in line, though. A simple "ahem" clearing of his throat was enough to make all the kids pipe down and jump into straight military-style lines. When Victor said, "Jump," everyone asked, "How high?"

By the end of our long day at the zoo, I was hot and tired, but Meghan and I still had the meeting to attend. I met Meghan in front of the Housing Authority offices in Torrance just in time. We were armed with the petition and ready to do whatever it took to get our project going.

During the meeting, it was my objective to make our intentions clear. We let them know about the petition with over 200 resident signatures, but didn't give it to them. We were saving it for higher authorities. The petition would be reserved for the Housing Authority's Executive Director.

As with most meetings with people representing any bureaucracy, I found the communication at this meeting to be particularly ambiguous and incongruent. All of a sudden, it felt like they were saying things they didn't really mean. All throughout the meeting, there seemed to be a lot of carefully placed, political maneuvering going on. And frankly, I didn't much trust the obsequious backslapping. They were being just too compliant and agreeable, which made it difficult to get a good feel for where they really stood. It just seemed too easy. We were getting our way, but it felt as though the people involved in our meeting were saying everything that we wanted to hear. Plus, they were very noncommittal. Conclusions, definites, and dates were completely avoided.

In spite of all the uncertainty, Meghan and I walked away believing that we were going to have the opportunity to involve the kids enrolled in the 4-H After-School Program and all the children in my class in a unique community service project. However, due to insurance restrictions, we were told that the children simply would not be able to be involved in the construction of the playground area. But, once the construction of the playground area was complete, the children would be allowed to beautify the surrounding area with trees, flowers, and other shrubbery supplied by HACLA.

Still feeling a little uncertain as to the definitiveness of our project, I figured it was time to send a letter and our petition to the guy on the top of the hierarchical management ladder—the Executive Director of the Housing Authority of Los Angeles. I wasn't certain what good it would do for our project, but as long as I had the petition and the signatures, I might as well send them in. Besides, I was still a little suspicious of the prior meeting with the Housing Authority. I couldn't believe that they were going to let us get involved that easily, especially after they put up such a fight in the beginning.

Here's the letter:

> Don J. Smith, Executive Director
> Housing Authority of the City of Los Angeles

2800 Wilshire Blvd.
Box 17157 Foy Station
Los Angeles, CA 90057

Dear Mr. Smith:

Some time ago I met you through the fence outside of Compton Avenue Elementary School. You were with a group of people from HACLA and two L.A. police officers surveying the area in preparation for the forthcoming modernization project. I was the teacher that inquired about your presence in the area. You may or may not remember me.

There are two reasons that I am writing to you. The first is to inform you of a project that I, and fellow educator Meghan McChesney, are attempting to facilitate at Compton Avenue School as it concerns the Hacienda Village housing development. The second is to ask for your assistance.

Basically, the project involves the children enrolled in the 4-H After-School Activity Program in the design and beautification of a playground area in Hacienda Village. Enclosed please find the preliminary proposal for the 4-H Community Service Project: *Caution: Children at Work.*

I have met with Allen O'Rourke, Assistant Director Housing Maintenance; Alfred Plummer, Construction Manager; and Sanford Riggs, Construction Support Supervisor. The meetings have been very encouraging and supportive. I am grateful for their assistance. I have also gathered the support of Deirdre Thompson, 4-H Youth Development Advisor. I have also gathered the support of Richard Linsey, President of the Hacienda Village Residents Advisory Council, and Lesa Woods, Community Liaison at Compton Avenue School and resident of Hacienda Village. And most importantly, I have assembled the support of approximately 200 Hacienda Village residents. Enclosed you will find the recently acquired petition of support.

As a result of our meetings with Sanford Riggs and the others, and with the residents' approval, we will begin to involve the children enrolled in the 4-H After-School Program in the design of the playground area at the western-most part of Hacienda Village. Richard Linsey and the Hacienda Village Residents Advisory Council will be holding a meeting at the Social Hall. At this meeting I will again present the ideas for our proposed project to the residents in order to gain their approval. Sanford Riggs has been invited to attend to meet the stipulated requirements of involving the residents in the modernization project.

As a concerned teacher and community member (I live on 107th Street and walk through Hacienda Village to and from work everyday), I believe that it is more than ever imperative that the residents and children be adequately involved in the rehabilitation and modernization project as it applies specifically to the upgrade of the playgrounds and tot lots in Hacienda Village. Truthfully, it is mostly because of my students that I have become involved. On a field trip through the area, my students expressed an interest in improving the playground areas, and I am trying to help them . . . help themselves.

If you could provide any assistance that would help to make what many believe to be a worthwhile project a reality, it would be greatly appreciated. I will call you next week to discuss this further. Thank you for your time and consideration on our behalf.

Sincerely,

John Gust

cc: Sylvia Ruiz, Principal
Richard Linsey
Deirdre Thompson

I called Mr. Smith about a week later and spoke to him on his car phone. I found him to be a very gracious, conscientious man. He was, in fact, very interested in our idea. And, since he did receive my letter and our petition, he was going to allow the children to design and beautify the playground area in Hacienda Village.

Caution: Children At Work!

Meghan named our project *Caution: Children At Work!* It became the first project ever, that involved inner-city children in the design of a playground built in a Housing and Urban Development community. In fact, the $80,000 playground became the largest of any in a public housing development in Los Angeles.

To guide the children through the process of designing their playground, we tried, as much as possible, to follow the premise of a student-directed curriculum. We had specific lessons to present and a few of our own ideas as to what we would like to do with the playground, but we wanted to let the design process flow and emerge in whichever way it might.

The first thing I did was to read to the 4-H'ers, the children's book *Miguel's Mountain,* by Bill Binzen. I wanted to introduce them to the idea of taking social action towards changing their community, and the book did a good job of it.

Miguel's Mountain is a story about a little boy and his efforts to save the large mound of dirt, or "mountain," that he and his friends played on in the middle of his city park. One day, while playing at the park, Miguel learned that the mountain was going to be leveled. City workers were going to come along with a bulldozer to flatten the hill. Because Miguel and his friends played on the mountain everyday, he was sad, and for the time being felt like there was nothing that he could do about it. Remaining awake in bed that night, Miguel thought long and hard about the mountain. Finally, in a creative burst of energy, he generated the idea of writing an authentic, purposeful, real-life letter to the mayor, asking him to save the mountain, which he and his friends loved. The next morning, with his mother's help, Miguel wrote and mailed the letter. After a few days of waiting nervously, Miguel was visited at home by a city official, who delivered the good news: "The mountain will stay right where it is forever!" the official said. Needless to say, Miguel was ecstatic. He and his friends, feeling listened to, empowered, important, and successful in their efforts, raced off to the park to celebrate on their mountain.

Once the 4-H'ers were as excited as Miguel was about the possibility of making a difference in *their* community, we went off to visit the playground site. While there, Meghan led the kids through various lessons, which started them on the way to becoming "real-life" architects. They drew pictures of what they saw at the playground, took photographs, measured the dimensions of the playground, and wrote in journals about what they saw.

Tory, who was in my classroom, wrote, "It's scummy. It smells and it's dirty."

"It looks like a total mess," wrote Tyrice, also from my classroom.

"I saw some monkey bars that are not working and polluted sand. The swings and the little horse are not painted," wrote fourth grader Luciana .

When we returned to the classroom, Meghan and I decided that we needed to find out what the children knew about the 4-H tradition. If the playground were going to be in the shape of a four-leaf clover, like the 4-H emblem, we needed to represent that tradition in our playground design. To do this, we brainstormed and clustered words that corresponded with, or represented, the four "H" themes of the 4-H tradition: head, heart, hands, and health.

Once the meaning or function of each of the four "H's" was gleaned, the children brainstormed what types of equipment or apparatus would best complement the established functions. For the head leaf, which symbolized clear thinking, the children thought it would be important to include clover leaf–shaped tables and surrounding benches for tutoring, homework, and mind-stimulating games. For the heart leaf, which symbolized sensitivity, the children wanted to place benches for adults to counsel and supervise small children. For the hands leaf, which symbolized helpfulness, the children wanted to place a garden to feed the hungry. And for the health leaf, which symbolized vitality, the children thought it would be important to include many different kinds of playground equipment and a physical fitness area for exercising.

Once an agreement was reached as to what should be represented by each leaf, the kids then worked in pairs in order to pre-draw their "ideal" four-leaf clover–shaped playground. For this pre-draw design, we gave them crayons and large pieces of construction paper with a four-leaf clover outline already drawn on it. This activity got them thinking about how they would, ideally, like to see the playground. It also helped to stimulate their creativity, as they were encouraged to draw whatever they liked.

With all of their creative, idealized, pre-draw designs completed, the 4-H'ers then got down to the serious business of once again becoming real-life architects. Meghan taught the children how to read architectural drawings, including roof plans, elevations, plans, and sections. She came up with the ingenious idea of using an apple as a manipulative with which to do this. After the kids cut up their apples according to Meghan's specifications, they got to eat them, too. They liked that. This groundwork enabled the children to work with the design kits provided by the company that manufactured the playground equipment that we were going to use for our playground.

As the children were becoming more and more experienced in architectural design, they were also visited by employees of HACLA. Sanford Riggs gave a slide presentation to show us what existing playgrounds at similar sites looked like. He also talked with the kids about the practicalities of playground design and the legal constraints set forth by Public Playground Safety. From Sanford, we learned that we couldn't use any tunnels in our designs, because, in the past, it had been discovered that homeless people would camp out or sleep in them. Apparently, the tunnels helped to protect them from the elements. We also learned that we had to limit the amount of chains that we used, because, in the past, people would steal the chains for various things, such as towing cars.

Once we understood our responsibilities, the children got down to the really challenging work. The 4-H'ers worked in small collaborative groups to create the playground's preliminary plans. This was a very difficult job.

Most of the kids had difficulty with this activity because it took a lot of time and attention to detail. But one young boy in particular started to shine. His name was Darin. A fifth grader, Darin quickly became the charismatic leader of the group showing people what to do and how to do it. It was amazing to watch him work with Meghan. It quickly became obvious that he was going to be the one to lead the group in the final design.

When the preliminary plans were completed, with Darin's leadership, we all put our heads together to create one final design. And what a design it was! The kids did a fabulous job.

One thing that we learned was that throughout the entire design process, instruction in architectural terms needed to be complemented with a broader lesson of teamwork and consensus building. It was time consuming, but the process of working in progressively larger groups definitely helped to promote consensus among all the participants. We all hoped that this resulting team spirit would serve as an insurance plan for shielding the new playground from the vandalism that ruined its predecessor. The last thing that we wanted to see was our playground looking like the one we saw when I first took my class through the housing community.

Architects Present

With the final design completed, Meghan and I prepared the kids for the presentation. We wanted the kids to look good for the dignitaries from the Housing Authority, 4-H, and Los Angeles Unified School District, and, of course, the residents of Hacienda Village.

For our presentation, we wanted to include the photographs, drawings, and journal entries of the 4-H'ers' first visit to the playground. That would help people to be aware of what it looked like currently. We also wanted to include the kids idealized pre-draw designs, the preliminary drawings, and, most importantly, the final design. This would let everyone know just how extensive a process designing the playground really was. Meghan also put together a slide show for the event so that everyone could more clearly see what we went through. And we also designed certificates of completion, which would be handed out to all the kids for their participation in the project.

Getting the kids ready and rehearsed for the event took a long time—as expected. They all had to know their parts, what they were supposed to do, what to say, and when to do it. When the time came, they were all in rare form. On the day of the presentation, they showed up at school all dressed up and looking good. Darin, who was accompanied by his mother, arrived in a sharp, double-breasted suit. Aside from the actual playground design, it was becoming obvious that he would be our main attraction.

Well in advance of our presentation, I invited as many people as I could think of. Invitations went out to all of the residents in Hacienda Village. I spent a lot of time canvassing Hacienda Village, passing out flyers, making sure everyone knew where the presentation would be held. I invited the Superintendent of the Ten Schools Project, Dr. Ted Alexander, but he didn't show. I also sent invitations to and called Maxine Waters, Mayor Reardon, councilman Rudy Svorinich, and councilwoman Rita Walters' offices. They didn't show either, but their representatives appeared in their place. Everyone from HACLA was, of course, invited, as were all the 4-H dignitaries. I even made sure to invite all the VISTA members who had helped out along the way.

When the big event finally arrived, inside our school's stuffy auditorium, the children explained their final architectural designs to HACLA and 4-H representatives, professors from UCLA, politicians, teachers, community members, and the press.

I thought the presentation was a great success. I MC'd the event, and Meghan led the kids through the presentation of the architectural design. The kids did a wonderful job. And, as expected, Darin was a big hit. In fact, he stole the show. He looked like a miniature Arsenio Hall up there describing our design process.

To finish our presentation, I called each of the 4-H'ers up one by one so that they could receive their certificates from the Executive Director of the Housing Authority, City of Los Angeles, Don Smith. They all looked so proud.

When everything was complete, Don Smith addressed the group, thanking the kids for all their help. And he invited us to host the dedication of the playground when the construction was completed. That was quite a surprise. Neither Meghan nor I expected that.

Later, when everyone was mingling around and parents were taking pictures, I found Don Smith so that I could personally thank him for giving us this opportunity. He, of course, was his usual gracious self, but then he said something that surprised me. He said, "Well, John, I really had no choice."

I didn't ask him, but I wondered if it were because of our persistence with all the meetings that we asked for, or if it were the petition that we organized, or if it were someone else, possibly from the 4-H organization or maybe even someone within HACLA, that had to do with his being forced into allowing us to redesign the playground. I never found out.

When the auditorium finally cleared, Meghan gave HACLA a copy of the final design. They in turn went back to their drawing boards, considered legal/regulatory constraints and completed the design of the community playground area. A few weeks later, HACLA presented the modifications to the residents in Hacienda Village, and with their approval, began construction of the playground.

All of our time-consuming work was finally done . . . for the time being, at least.

Meghan Moves In

At long last, someone from the Teach For America organization decided to take the spare bedroom. No one else from TFA had even so much as given a call. Absolutely no inquiries.

I thought that perhaps my advertisement in the newsletter had been written in a tone that was both too challenging and too confrontational, for the TFA audience. And because of that, I feared, no one dared give me a call. I did have a tendency to be a little too candid about my thoughts and feelings. And to some people, I'm sure this made me a little too brusque or laconic to be around.

But then again, it could be that no one—except for Meghan—had the courage, the compassion, or the raw desire that was needed to make the commitment to move into the Watts community. Or, it could be that no one—except for Meghan—thought it was important enough to do so. Or simply, because all the Teach For America teachers were in their first two years of teaching, they believed that was enough to worry about, without also having to take on the additional challenge of embedding themselves in the community where they worked.

I was so very glad that Meghan was my friend. Without her intelligent and insightful input and involvement, I know I never would have been able to move into the community myself, or bring the playground project to fruition, or complete the teacher resource book that I had been contracted to write. And she did all of this, in just her first year of teaching!

Meghan was more than just a constant source of support and encouragement. In many ways, she was the brainchild behind many of our interventions. If I had not known that she had former experience in playground design and development from her undergraduate work in architecture, and had she not made it clear prior to my stumbling upon the playground in Hacienda Village that she had wanted to implement a project while in Los Angeles that involved children in the architectural design and construction of a playground, I never would have thought about facilitating the renovation of the playground in the first place. Basically, even though it needed to be my students' idea, it was really her idea all along. Yes, my class did happen upon the deteriorated playground in Hacienda Village, and yes, they did express the desire to renovate the playground, but my conversations with Meghan beforehand more than likely influenced the dialogue I had with my students.

And because Meghan had interest in community development, urban planning, and architecture, and had ideas as to how to involve children in all of that, while also totally involving herself as an equal participant of the community, she decided to move in. Meghan had a keen mind, a great set of values, and a limitless source of energy. So, I am certain that in spite of all of my confrontational challenges, Meghan moved into the spare bedroom totally of her own volition and accord. She was as independent a thinker and mover as I had ever come across. And I was damn glad to know her.

Thinking About God?

"You've heard from all of us. Now what do you think about God, Mr. Gust?" When Raynell first asked this question, I shook. It felt like breaking hard ground.

I had been able to convince the class to read the fifth grade-level book *The Sign of the Beaver,* by Elizabeth Spears. I felt that they were ready for it—

overall, my class' reading level was extremely high. And they all liked the idea of reading a book that fifth graders typically read. It made them feel proud and mature to be reading such a long-chapter book.

Reading the book together, we had just come to the part where Matt, the twelve-year-old Caucasian boy who was left alone to take care of his family's homestead, was telling Attean, the slightly older Native American boy whose people had always lived in the woodlands, the biblical story of Noah and the ark.

Our classmate Steven knew the story well. He did an excellent job of clarifying Matt's version of the story for the class. He explained, "With the great flood, God wiped out all the bad people on Earth but saved Noah and his good family."

And as we continued reading, Attean retorted with a similar story specific to his culture. "Very long time," Attean began, scowling as he tried to translate from his own tongue, "before animal, was great rain. Water came over all the land. One Indian go to very high hill, climb very high tree. Rain many days. Water come up to feet of Indian, but no more. Gluskabe bring three ducks to Indian. One day he let one duck go. It fly away and not come back. Then last duck come back with mud in mouth. Indian know water go down. When water all gone, he come down from tree. He make grass. Make bird and animal. Make man and beaver. Man and beaver make all other Indians."

I think all of us were enjoying our lesson in cultural mythology that late morning.

And even before this discussion about Noah and Attean's peoples' version of the story, generated from the book we were reading, conversations about God were beginning to arise more and more in the classroom as the end of the year approached. And the question, "What is God?" had still not been crossed off as answered from the long list of questions that the children had generated earlier. Somehow I had managed to avoid addressing this question, but now, it was obvious that its time had come.

In the kids' comments or conversations about God, I had noticed that they had been calling God "He." I figured that representation was fine and well, but at the same time, I always wondered how we came to imagine God to be of human form. Our culture's anthropocentrism never ceased to puzzle me. Like a scientist, perhaps, I wanted to know what gave the kids the impression that God was a "He." Was it an idea generated individually in each child's mind? Or was it an idea that their parents, our culture, or social constructs taught them? My inclination was to believe that it was the latter.

Since I *was* asked by Raynell, I felt obligated to provide an answer, but first I had a few questions of my own. "First of all," I said, "I keep wondering why all of you think God is a 'He.' Why don't you call God, 'She'? Or for that matter, why don't you call God, 'It'? I guess I want to know because lots of people in different parts of the world, and even some people right here in Los

Angeles, think of God as many different kinds of things. Some people even call God by a different name. Some people use names like Allah or Atman or Brahman, or the Tao. Some people call God Nirvana, Budda-nature, the Void, Absolute Subjectivity, or even Ultimate Reality."

Steven who was really into superheroes and professional wrestling asked, "Kinda like the Ultimate Warrior, huh, Mr. Gust?"

After all the giggles and murmuring subsided, I said, while also trying to hide my own smile, "No, I don't think so, Steven. I don't think it's quite the same." Then I continued, "Some people even think that there are many Gods. And some people think there is no God at all."

Roberta shook her head and said, "Nuh-uh, there is too a God."

I paused for a moment and then asked, "I wonder what Matt and Attean in our story think about God. Do you think they think of God as a 'He'? Or do they think of something else when they think of God? And what do Attean's people think about God? They call their God Gluskabe, don't they? None of us really knows much about what Attean and his people think or believe about God, do we?"

They all shook their heads no, while becoming aware that we were about to set off on another tangent of literature-inspired inquiry.

For a moment I thought I was going to get away with not answering Raynell's question, but Raynell wasn't going to let me get off that easy, "Yeah, but Mr. Gust, you still haven't told us about what you think of God."

I was a little concerned, because I didn't know for sure how to explain. I was afraid that the way I was beginning to think about God was probably so very different from what they thought about God. And I really didn't want to confuse them. You see, my thinking was that God was not apart from the world. The perception of the dualistic otherness of God was no longer a part of my worldview. For me, God is transcendent, yes, but also imminent. God is an observer and a participant. I didn't think that God constructed our world, our solar system, our galaxy, or our universe like some kind of complex machine with a set of unchanging laws or rules, which kept it running, and then severed Himself from the creation so that it could run on its own. I believed that we—or everything, for that matter—are immersed and imbedded within God. Divinity permeates all. God is boundless and we are all a part of It, Him, or Her. In other words, God is an all-pervasive creative source and shines through everything.

While thinking about God, and how I would explain my perception of God to the children, I also began to wonder if this were an entirely feeble task. How could God—even though intimately close—become something that could ever really be thought about. Because, no matter what I, or we, thought or imagined, God would always be so much more.

So after making an effort to think on it, I told them, "For me, personally, I think God is a He, a She, and an It. For me, God is everything and is everywhere. God is both out there, up there in the sky, looking down at us, and in here." I placed my hand on my chest, pausing for a moment. "God is every feeling and thought we have. God is everything we do. God is you and I."

"God is watching us and playing along with us at the same time. God is everything—hard things like the floor and this desk that I'm sitting on, and really soft things like the air all around us. God is the sky, the moon, the stars, the clouds, and . . . your mothers."

I then looked over at Yaquese, who had been hurt recently when Roberta made fun of her extremely dark skin, and said, "God is also in you and your skin, with all its beautiful colors. God is everything."

Then I pulled a quarter out of my pocket, held it up for the class to see, and said, "You see, I think God is a He, a She and an It, because, to me, God is just like this coin. This coin, as all of you know, has one side that we call 'heads' and another side that we call . . ."

"Tails," interrupted Roberta.

"That's right, Roberta," I continued. "To me, you could call the sides He and She instead of head and tails. Therefore, God is both sides of the coin. To me, there is nothing that is not God. To me, God is black and white, cold and hot, outside and inside, life and death, good and bad, everything and . . . well, nothing. And if you think about it really, or just think of this coin that I'm still holding, God is It, too. God is the whole thing, not just one side."

I was somewhat surprised when a large majority of the class disagreed with me. Yaquese in particular was sure that God was a "He." Perhaps some omnipotent, white-bearded man standing on a cumulus cloud up high in the sky somewhere, keeping watch over her. This personal, patriarchal God seemed to provide a sense of security for her, and I certainly didn't want to upset her in anyway, so I told the class, "Well, I'm glad that all of you know what God is. And it's good that you believe the way you do! I certainly don't want you to go changing the way you believe or think about God. I just told you all what I think and believe about God, because Raynell asked. So don't forget, each of us is entitled to think or believe whatever we want about God. And there's nothing that anybody can do to make any of you change your mind."

Then, just as I was finishing up telling the class my thoughts on God, the bell rang. Time for lunch. The kids put away their books and lined up at the door. I, of course, walked with them to the cafeteria and dropped them off to eat.

Later that day, after school, when I got home, I told Meghan about our conversation about God in the classroom. After my somewhat lengthy explanation, Meghan asked, "Can you do that? Can you talk about God in the classroom?"

At the time, in the classroom, I really didn't think about whether I could or not. All I knew was that Raynell wanted to know what I thought. And as a teacher, I wasn't in the habit of not telling my students things, not sharing information. My natural inclination was to teach, to answer questions. Plus, I pretty much knew I was in the clear because I was only telling them about what *I* thought about God. I certainly didn't tell them how *they* should think about God. At most, all I was doing was exposing them to another perspective.

I knew of the First Amendment's guarantee of freedom of religion and its prohibition of any government establishment of religion. I even knew some of the words of that amendment: "Congress shall make no law respecting an establishment of religion, or prohibiting the free exercise thereof" I also knew that I could protect my students' right to spiritual expression. And I knew that this concerned the extent to which they could learn about religion and express their own religious convictions in our public schools.

I was not allowed to provide any kind of religious instruction in the classroom, but I was allowed to teach about the Bible in the teaching of history or literature, for example. But that was just the Judeo-Christian view. From what I knew, the public school system in our country did very little to really acknowledge the many other religions or spiritual traditions. The only way I ever heard the other ways of thinking and practicing being addressed was as "other scriptures." So, what about the other Semitic religion, Islam, and the Koran? And what about Hinduism and the Upanishads and Vedas, or Buddhism and the Tipitaka, or Sikhism and the Janamsakhi stories, or Confucianism and the Analects, or Taoism and the collection of meditations called the Tao Te Ching? What about learning about those religions and their scriptures? And what about Jainism, Mencius, Shinto, and Xunzi? I didn't know a thing about those. And what about mythology and the various indigenous cultures around the world? And what about any other religions that I might not have known about at all? Why were so few people in our country aware of these religions or philosophies, and their resulting worldviews?

I also knew that I was allowed to teach civic values and virtue, and the moral code that binds us together as a community, so long as I remained neutral with respect to the promotion of any particular religion. But I wasn't sure what any of these regulations or guarantees had to do with my students' spiritual needs, growth, and development.

Throughout all my efforts to identify my worldview and personal philosophy of education—and determining my thoughts and beliefs about God was certainly very much a part of that task—my viewpoint of the learner was also becoming very clear. For me, a student arrived in my classroom as a whole, complete human being. They didn't enter my classroom and then reach into their skulls to place their brain—their cognition or intellect—on a desk and then walk out of the room, carrying with them the rest of their domains (physical, emotional, social, intuitive, aesthetic, and spiritual). A human being cannot be fragmented into parts! Therefore, I was coming to believe that the child, as a whole, must always be addressed.

And if I were to go a little further to consider the larger context within which the whole human being was embedded, I would have to say that it was spiritual. To me, yes, we are just an insignificant biological entity and infinitesimal part of this spiritual context, this universe. But we are also something much more than all that. In some way that I certainly wasn't able to explain, I believed that we held within us all the data regarding all of existence and the entire universe. And being inherently spiritual in nature then, we therefore also had the potential to experientially access all of this spiritual context. Therefore, I believed, when educating the whole human being, the realization of our divine union with this all-pervading spirit, experienced as eternal happiness, should be our true, ultimate end or purpose.

"Wannabes"

While eating a bowl of cereal before going to school one morning, I decided to step outside onto my front porch to get some fresh air and see what the weather was like. As I walked out onto the porch, I noticed that there was something spray painted on the concrete near the steps. My house had been tagged! During the night, someone apparently had been sitting on the front porch and, while smoking a couple of cigarettes—two cigarette butts were also left there—they spray-painted their tag on the concrete. The unfamiliar marking looked like this:

E HVB1
S ₵K
Smokey

I felt a little uneasy about the tagging. I didn't like the whole idea of someone sitting on the porch late at night smoking cigarettes. Why were they there? Were they getting ready to do something more? Did they have a beef or something? Did they just want to let us know that they were there and could do almost anything they wanted to do whenever they wanted? Or were they just walking by and because they were tired, decided to sit down to take a rest and have a smoke? Anyway, I didn't like it, but there wasn't much that could be done about it. At least, not then; it was time to go to work.

After all the kids were in the classroom, after reciting the pledge of allegiance to the flag, and after listening to all the morning announcements over the intercom system, I decided to ask the kids about the tagging. I wanted to know what it meant, and I knew they could give me all the answers.

Silently, I walked over to the chalkboard, slowly picked up a piece of chalk and drew the marking on the board. Making a deliberate attempt to appear dramatic, I turned around to face the class, looked at them intensely, and asked, "Can anyone tell me what this means?"

Hands shot up all over the room. Apparently, most everyone could tell me something about the tagging. Taking the time to think about who to pick, I scanned the room and chose Donnell.

Donnell knew everything about the tag mark. He even knew the guy that left it!

He explained that the E slash S meant "Eastside," the HVB was the abbreviation for the local gang, called the Hacienda Village Boys, and the little number 1 by the B meant "number 1" (as, in the best). He also explained that the CK with the crossed out C meant "Crypt Killer." And Smokey was the street name of the person from the neighborhood who did the tagging. In fact, Donnell explained, it was the guy that was sitting in the passenger seat of the lowrider that flew by my house at about fifty miles per hour, bouncing three to four feet in the air, while I was sitting on my front porch talking with James, Jamal, and Donnell a week earlier.

I don't know why I was surprised about Donnell's ability to tell me everything about the tagging. He was already a wise old man of the streets. I guess it was in the way he said it. So matter of factly, like it was just an everyday part of his life. Nothing special, but pretty cool. That's how they saw it—all of my students. At the same time, they all appeared to be somewhat irritated with my ignorance. They couldn't believe that I didn't understand. I got that, "Can you believe this guy? He doesn't know" look.

In spite of their impatience with my ignorance, I sensed an opportunity for a more in-depth conversation about the topic. I kept probing. And the kids kept answering. They told me everything I wanted to know. I found out about the little cliques within the "Bloods" gang in the area. The boys, and some of the girls, told me about the "Bonnie Hannas" clique, the "WRB" or "RBM" clique, the "Circles" or "CCP" clique, and the "Haciendas" or "HVB" clique. And then there were the Eastside HVB's, Southside HVB's and 107th Street HVB's monikers. Boy, was I getting an education.

After discussing gang nicknames, streetnames, or monikers and what they meant, I asked if any of my students had a nickname. I discovered that Donnell was also known as "Little Pi Ru" or "Red Nose," that James was called "Little Benzo," and that Jobay's alias was "Little Jo Vani."

I couldn't believe it. Here were my little "innocent" second and third graders, and some of them already had gang streetnames. What was going to happen to them when they got older? I wanted to know. So I asked them, "How many of you here want to be in gang? What do you call it . . . 'Wannabes'? How many of you are Wannabes?"

Every single one of the boys' hands when up. Well, everyone except for Raynell. Thank goodness. I stood there not really believing what I was seeing. I didn't know what to say. This was to be their big ambition in life? To be a full-fledged gang member? And what kind of dirty deeds would they have to complete to earn the right to no longer be just a "Wannabe." Was there some sort of invented "rite of passage" full of an abundance of destructive tasks that they had to achieve before finally making it into the gang?

The interesting thing was that, during our reading of *The Sign of the Beaver*, it was apparent that Attean, the Native American adolescent of the story, was himself a "Wannabe." For some time, Attean had been attempting to show his worth or appear useful to his elders, in an effort to be allowed to go on the great hunt. And now he was getting ready to enter into his own rite of passage—some test that would ultimately prove he had earned the right to be one of them.

But this rite of passage was something that the responsible elders had been requiring of its youth probably since the culture's inception! After his grandfather put Attean through a period of fasting and extensive preparation and training, which I gathered would serve to foster some nonordinary state of consciousness, he was to go out into the forest alone, so that he could find his manitou, or "spirit."

In the story, Attean himself explained to Matt that his spirit might come to him in a dream as some kind of animal, tree, or voice. And if it did arise as a human voice, he would be quite lucky, too, because, as Attean explained, most of the time these spirit guides didn't communicate to people in words.

Well, as the story progresses, Attean does go out into the forest alone and he does find his manitou. And when Attean is accompanied by his grandfather in a later visit to Matt, it is clearly noticeable to Matt that Attean has changed. Standing taller and straighter, beaming with pride, Attean had indeed become a man. He had earned the right and privilege of going on the big hunt with his elders—the gang, if you will. He had found his manitou, his spirit.

I couldn't help wondering why we in our day and age never thought of doing such things. Why didn't we make more of an effort to provide a meaningful rite of passage for our youth? A rite of passage that fostered the finding of the spirit. Why didn't we, as Attean's culture did, attempt to facilitate truly transformative learning experiences by making an effort to become aware of, accept and appreciate the symbolic contents of our unconscious?

It just seemed to make sense for our elders to also provide our youth, like Attean, with an opportunity to have a truly meaningful and transcendent, subjective inner experience—perhaps as a result of some predesigned rite of passage. And, it was obvious to me that our youth also thought so. Due to our neglect or short-sightedness, the youth of today, as a result of some unexpressed need, felt a need to create a rite of passage of their own. Too bad it was only for getting into a gang.

Murder on the Block

One afternoon during lunch, Jim, one of the guys that I had met while walking through Hacienda Village, came into my classroom. Jim was one of Victor's brothers. I was in the classroom with Tyronda and Kristie. They were helping rinse out all the milk cartons that we had been saving. We were going to plant some seeds in the cartons later that afternoon. Eventually, after the plants became fully grown, we were going to transplant them to the Hacienda Village playground, which was now under construction.

When I first met Jim, he was one of the guys that used to hang out with all the other unemployed men in the parking lot of Hacienda Village. But today, his time was limited. He, too, was on his lunch break. He came into the classroom to personally thank me for helping him get a job!

When I first saw him, I could barely make out who he was. He was walking down the somewhat dark hallway towards our classroom. As he was silhouetted against the walls of the hallway, I knew he wasn't anyone that was working at our school, but I also knew he was someone familiar. He shouted at me, saying, "Hey, John, how's it going?"

I looked closer and, with the help of his voice, knew exactly who it was. "Hey, Jim," I said. "What's up?"

He came into the classroom wearing workboots and a light green uniform. On his shirt pocket was a patch that said "Housing Authority."

"I just wanted to come in to thank you for helping to get me a job," he said.

"You're working now?" I asked. "For the Housing Authority? No shit!"

Realizing that I had just sworn, I quickly turned to see if Tyronda and Kristie, who were still busy cleaning milk cartons at the sink, had noticed. Luckily for me, they too were busy talking.

Jim continued, "Yeah, if it hadn't been for you and that playground they're building over there, I wouldn't be working. Anyway, I just wanted to come in and let you know and thank you."

I didn't have the heart to tell him that I really had nothing to do with his getting the job. The Housing Authority was planning to build a new playground regardless of anything I had to do with it. I was only able to get the Housing Authority to allow the kids to complete the architectural design of the playground.

No matter how inaccurate I thought Jim's announcement was, it had to be one of the highlights of my year. I mean, I had to admit, I was pretty excited about the playground and all, but up until Jim came into the room, the whole playground just didn't seem to have much impact on me. Sure, it was becoming a great experience for the kids, and they were learning a lot, but it didn't seem to have much affect on the surrounding community. Hearing all of this from one person, Jim, made all the difference in the world. Plus, later, when I told Victor about what his brother had done and said, and how I felt that I didn't really have anything to do with it, he said, "John, you had a lot more to do with it than you know." This made me very happy.

The day after Jim's visit, at about 7:00 AM, as I was walking through Hacienda Village, I made sure to check out the playground site. In a way, it sort of felt like my playground. I knew it wasn't, but going there to look at the sight sort of felt like going to look over the progress the builders have made when you have bought a new house. By this time, all the old playground equipment was gone and the ground was all torn up. About three construction trucks were there, and two men were looking over some blueprints at the back end of one of the trucks. I looked for Jim, but he wasn't there. Maybe it was too early yet, or maybe he was going to be working at a different site; I didn't know. I did know, however, that I was feeling extremely happy that I had something to do with all of this—no matter how little.

By Wednesday morning of that week, I pulled myself out of bed at 4:30 AM. I needed to do some work on the teacher resource book that Meghan and I were *still* busy writing. I quickly turned on the computer and went into the kitchen to make some coffee. After the coffee had finished brewing, I grabbed a cup and walked back to my office, opened up the file that I needed, and got to work.

I had been working for about ten minutes when I heard a gunshot, a woman's scream, and then two more shots! It was close, too. Closer than any other gunshots I had ever heard before.

When it happened, I wasn't nervous and I wasn't scared—at least I don't think I was. When I heard the shots and the scream originally, I took notice of it, but I didn't do anything. I didn't stop typing, I didn't go outside, I didn't call the police. I just kept on writing.

I just ignored the whole incident and kept on with my work. Either I was totally oriented towards completing my task—which was a definite possibility—or I just didn't much care. Perhaps I was becoming as lethargic, apathetic, and fearful as some of my neighbors.

I recalled the conversation that I had with James' stepfather after I found out that James had witnessed a murder at the end of our street. He said, "Nothing new, no big deal." I guess I was beginning to feel that way, too. Maybe I was just accepting all the insanity of it, knowing that there wasn't anything I could do about it. Then again, maybe my reaction, or lack of it, was nothing more than a measure of self-protection. Maybe the only way to cope with everything that happened in this neighborhood was to deny that it ever happened. Ignore it.

When it happened, though, I didn't want to go outside because I didn't know exactly what was happening. I certainly didn't want to get in the middle of anything. A few minutes later, I heard a couple of cars driving down the street. I didn't look to see what kind of cars they were, but my guess was that they were police cars. Then I heard a police siren coming down the street. But I still didn't get off the computer to take a look at what was going on. After that, I heard yet another vehicle coming down the street. This time it sounded like a large truck. That's when I leaned over and looked out the door of my little study to notice a huge fire truck and an ambulance coming down the street. Only then did I decide to take a break from my writing.

When I walked out to the sidewalk, the night was still pitch black. I noticed that quite a few cop cars, about four or five, were down the street, with their lights going. I decided to take a walk down to see what all the commotion was. When I got close enough, I noticed that the street was already taped off with the long yellow tape that police use to mark off a crime scene. A body was lying on the curb and a group of paramedics were leaning over it. I strained to get a closer look, but I couldn't make out if the person were dead or alive. As the paramedics were examining the man or woman, I didn't know which, a policewoman approached me. She asked if I saw or heard anything.

Before I answered her, I first asked if someone got shot. What a dumb question to ask. Of course someone got shot; why else would they be there! Polite police officer that she was, she said yes, of course. Then I asked her if the guy were dead. She didn't know. With my questions answered, I then told her that I heard a gunshot, a loud scream, and then two more gunshots, but that I didn't see anything. She took down my name, address, phone number, and date of birth and then went about the business of looking in the bushes around the houses close by. I guessed that she was probably looking for a gun or something.

When the paramedics zipped up a body bag and walked away from the body lying there on the curb, I knew it was over. I went back into my house, turned off the computer, and simply got ready for work. Nothing I could do. End of story, I thought.

I didn't even think about it. I just put the whole incident out of my mind. Just as natural as ever, I walked to the bathroom, turned on the shower, took my shower, ironed my clothes, got dressed, ate my breakfast, brushed my teeth, made my lunch, packed my backpack, and left the house. Nothing new, just another day.

When I walked out of the house, I don't know why but I was somewhat surprised to see Mr. Watkins across the street, standing on his porch looking in the direction of the murder scene. I looked down the street and noticed that the police were still there. I also noticed that several other neighbors were standing on their front porches, looking on. I guess I expected the whole incident to be completely over. You know: body packed up and hauled off, blood stains washed away, and nothing more mentioned of the whole affair. Maybe, unconsciously, that's what I really wanted. I didn't want to deal with it anymore. But here it was, still staring me in the face. Great way to start off my Wednesday.

I walked across the street to talk to Mr. Watkins. He looked sad. That was the only time I ever saw him like that. He looked like he was about to cry. I told him that I heard the shots and a woman's scream this morning around 5 AM. I asked if he knew who it was. He slowly turned to me, looked at me straight with his own tear-filled eyes, and said, "It was my godchild's mother."

I didn't know what to say. I just stood there. Inside I was saying, "Oh my God! I don't want to deal with this. I just want it to be over and forgotten." Outside I said, "I'm so sorry, Mr. Watkins."

He didn't look back. He just kept looking in the direction of the taped-off crime scene. Just then, his godchild, a grown woman who was sitting in the passenger side of a Jeep Cherokee, accompanied by several other people in the vehicle, rode by. She had her head back and her hands over her eyes. She was screaming and crying and kicking. Mr. Watkins watched her driving by, too. I stood there watching Mr. Watkins.

I had to get out of there. Not knowing what else to do, I set off in the direction of the crime scene. I didn't want to, but I had to go that way to get to work. I thought about going in the other direction for a moment, and even started to walk that way, but it would have taken so much longer to get to work. Plus, I think some small trace of curiosity got the best of me. That's pretty sick, really. Human nature, I guess.

When I reached the taped-off area, I met up with Lavell, Donnell, James, and a few other kids that I didn't quite know. I nodded hello, looked at their faces, and kept walking. I didn't say anything. I didn't tell them to leave and go to school: I didn't ask them how they were feeling, nothing. I just kept walking. I guess I didn't know what to do. I was stunned. The whole street was silent. It felt eerie.

As I passed by the crime scene, most of the uniformed cops standing around looked at me. And they kept looking. They might have been wondering what a white man wearing a tie and carrying a backpack would be doing in this neighborhood walking down the street past a murder scene. I didn't say anything to them either. I just kept walking.

When I reached Hacienda Village, a row of people were standing on the sidewalk, watching. Guy, one of the younger fellows that I met when I was encountered on one of my first trips through Hacienda Village, was there looking on. His daughter was a kindergarten student at Compton Avenue. I said hello, stopped for a moment to look back, and kept walking. Mary, a woman I met when we petitioned Hacienda Village for the playground, was also standing nearby. I nodded to her and kept walking. As I walked by, she explained to another woman standing there that I was a teacher at Compton Avenue and that I lived on 107th Street. Obviously, the woman had a hard time believing it. She kept looking at me in disbelief.

When I got to school, the day went by pretty much according to plan. My class and I started working on the little patch of dirt, right outside of my classroom, that ran along the fence off of Compton Avenue. We were going to plant some ferns and, hopefully, grow some flowers in the area. And once our plants became full grown and healthy, we had plans to transfer them over to the playground in Hacienda Village.

I taught the kids how to use the gardening tools that a fellow teacher brought to school. We had several back hoes, rakes, shovels, and a pick ax. Our job for the day, aside from the kids learning how to use the tools, was to overturn the dirt to get it ready for planting. We had a great time doing it, too. I loved getting kids involved in hands-on learning. It sure beat the heck out of the constant drudge of paper, pencils, and books.

Feeling pretty good about our busy and productive day, which kept me from thinking about the murder, I walked into the office to sign out and go home. Mrs. Ruiz took me aside and asked me to put a hold on the work outside for a while. Seems she had been told by the school police, local police, or housing authority police, I'm not sure which, that there had been a number of random drive-by shootings going on lately. Gangsters had been shooting up houses and housing development units for no apparent reason. Understandably, she wanted me to keep my students inside until the shooting died down. I was disappointed but willing to abide by her wishes.

She knew nothing about the murder that I had heard that morning, so I decided not to compound her worries and told her nothing.

After I finished talking with Mrs. Ruiz, I decided to walk home and take a look at the progress of the playground. And I wanted to find Jim to say hello. When I reached the playground area, I noticed that most of the workmen were still there, but they were getting ready to finish up for the day.

Jim came up to me and gave me a closed-fist handshake. I didn't know exactly what kind of handshake he was looking for, so I hit his fist head on. Then I clumsily tried to hit his fist again from the bottom and stuck my fist out, thinking he was going to do the same to mine. He didn't and I felt stupid. I always was clumsy with nontraditional handshakes. Jim didn't seem to care, though. That was a relief.

I asked him if he had heard anything about the shooting this morning and, of course, he had. He told me that the word out was that the woman's son was involved in a drug deal that went bad. Figures. Apparently, the son living at the home sold three kilos of cocaine to someone for 27K each. That's $81,000! And it was all bad. The murderers were just dishing out their form of retribution for the bad deal. Maybe it was just some type of task required as a rite of passage into a gang. I could only speculate. Heck of a trade, I guess—$81,000 in exchange for your mother's life.

I continued on my walk through Hacienda Village until I came out at 107th Street. When I reached the street, I noticed that Mr. Watkins' god child, the daughter of the murder victim, and a grown woman with a child of her own, was sitting on the front porch, surrounded by several other people. I crossed the street right in front of their house and almost went up to them to tell them how sorry I was. But for some reason, probably because I didn't know them and because I really didn't do too well in those kinds of situations, (maybe nobody really does), I just kept walking.

I made it home safely, closed my door, and locked it tight.

Darin Goes to Washington

Typically, when I arrived home from work, the first thing I did, after unlocking the doors, of course, was to check my messages. I didn't have to check for bugs anymore, they were all gone. And I no longer ran to the back of the house to make sure nobody had gotten in. I was becoming more comfortable with the house and the neighborhood.

A few days after the murder, when I arrived home, I received a voice mail from Deirdre Thompson of the 4-H office. She called to inform me that Darin, the fine young man that did such an excellent job of explaining our architectural design to Don Smith, the Executive Director of the Housing Authority of the City of Los Angeles, and the rest of the dignitaries in our school's auditorium, was going to be flown to Washington to explain the *Caution: Children At Work!* program to the Secretary of the U. S. Department of Housing and Urban Development, Henry G. Cisneros.

Whoa! I was stoked! Our project was going to be presented personally by one of our participants to the Secretary of the U. S. Department of Housing and Urban Development—Henry Cisneros himself! What a great opportunity for Darin!

The 4-H After-School Programs in Kansas City, Oakland, Philadelphia, and Los Angeles were to share a $3.5 million HUD grant, and Darin was going there to help explain the accomplishments and successes of the 4-H After-School Program in Los Angeles.

All Deirdre wanted us to do was to put together a portfolio and help prepare Darin for his presentation. Meghan, the great resource that she was, helped me prepare the portfolio. All we needed to do was to make a few color copies of our architectural boards, write up a brief synopsis to be placed in the front of the portfolio, and include copies of the articles that appeared in the *Los Angeles Times*, the *L.A. Watts Times* and *La Opinion* newspapers about our project. Piece of cake.

As for Darin, well, being as sharp as he was, I knew preparing him for the presentation would be just as easy. And it was. I went up to his classroom and asked his teacher if I could borrow him during his lunch time so that we could go over the plans for his presentation. No problem. Darin, responsible as always, came by my classroom, ready to go. He was excited about the opportunity to go to Washington. You could see it in his eyes! Such a bright fifth grader.

He sat down in the room and I showed him the portfolio that Meghan and I had prepared, and we went through it and reviewed all the things that we had done.

Darin remembered everything. I explained to him our little summary of the project, which I placed in the front of the portfolio, and then showed him the articles from the newspapers. He already knew about the article from the *Los Angeles Times*; in fact, he could show me the exact locations in the article where his name was mentioned, and recite verbatim what he was quoted saying, "A lot of kids our age are dying. We don't want that to happen. So we decided to make it safe," and "The gangbangers may try and take it down again. But if they do . . . I hope we can have the same fun to build it up again." But he didn't know about the articles in the *L.A. Watts Times* and *La Opinion* newspapers. He was excited to learn about those. A picture of Darin in his double-breasted suit appeared in the article in the *L.A. Watts Times.* I could tell he was proud.

After I felt Darin was adequately prepared, I shook his hand, congratulated him, told him how proud I was of him, wished him well, told him to have fun but behave himself, and sent him on his way. With the portfolio safely tucked away in his backpack, Darin left my classroom and headed straight for the playground.

At the end of the day, after signing out in our front office, I ran into Mrs. Ruiz. I briefed her on Darin and his pending trip to Washington. She already knew about the trip; she had been told the day before by Deirdre Thompson from 4-H. Mrs. Ruiz seemed to be as excited as I was.

On my way home, as usual, I stopped by the playground area to check on the progress. I walked on the clover-leaf shaped sidewalk that was already in place, all the way around to the back of the playground. The construction crew had just finished putting in the forms that would hold the concrete for the raised rose garden that the kids decided to include in the design.

Monday, when I returned to work, I found Darin at the 4-H After-School Activity Program. He told me all about his trip. He was so excited. Yes, he did get to speak with Cisneros. I was so glad. Actually, he met with Cisneros at a press conference. He told Cisneros all about our project and was also interviewed by reporters from CBS and ABC. There were cameras there and everything! He showed Cisneros the portfolio that Meghan and I had prepared and told him all about the program and pictures. Darin said that Cisneros was a very nice man, who had to leave early in order to attend his son's soccer game.

Darin went on about his trip. While in Washington, he also had the opportunity to take in the sights. He saw the State Capital, the White House, the Washington Monument, the Lincoln Memorial, and the Tomb of the Unknown Soldier. Darin also saw President Clinton as he was walking toward his limousine. "I shouted out to him, but he just kept on walking," Darin said.

"Well," I said, "if I were you, Darin, I wouldn't worry about it too much. The way you're going, you might just have Mr. Clinton calling on you before too long."

Later, I discovered that during his speech at the press conference, Mr. Cisneros was quoted saying, "The accomplishments of the 4-H After-School Program in Los Angeles have inspired us to help it expand. The unprecedented collective effort of individuals, government, public education, and business has made a difference in the lives of the nearly 1,200 children this program has touched so far in Los Angeles alone. I anticipate that as the 4-H After-School Program is developed in Oakland, Kansas City, and Philadelphia, leaders from other cities will look at them and Los Angeles as models for success." Way to go 4-H!

I also saw a picture of Darin holding the giant $500,000 check the U. S. Department of Housing and Urban Development provided to expand the 4-H After-School Activity Program in Los Angeles. Good job, Henry! All right, Darin!

That evening, Meghan and I decided that Cisneros deserved a letter thanking him for taking the time out of his busy day to meet with Darin and the other participants in the 4-H program. We wrote the letter and sent it off the following day.

Henry Cisneros, Secretary
U. S. Department of Housing and Urban Development
451 Seventh Street, S.W.
Washington, D.C. 20410

Dear Mr. Cisneros:

We would like to extend to you our heartfelt thanks for taking the time out of your busy schedule to meet with Darin.

As you may well remember, Darin was the fifth grade student enrolled in the 4-H After School Activity Program at Compton Avenue Elementary

School in Los Angeles who presented the *Caution: Children At Work!* program to you on his recent visit to Washington. To refresh your memory, this was the student designed playground that is currently being constructed in Hacienda Heights Housing and Urban Development community in Watts. Darin was instrumental in helping to make the program a success.

Before he left for Washington, Darin was extremely excited over the possibility of meeting with you. This was Darin's first time in an airplane. So you can imagine what flying cross-country to Washington with the possibility of speaking with you meant for Darin. Actually, we were all keeping our fingers crossed hoping that Darin would be able to meet with you. Simply, we wanted Darin to experience meeting with such a prominent political figure and role model as yourself.

We all wish nothing but the best for Darin, as we believe that one day this fine young man may actually be helping to improve the country in the way that you are doing at this time. Thank you once again for your generosity and compassion for those who so desperately need it. You are to be commended.

Sincerely,

John Gust
Compton Avenue Elementary School
Los Angeles Unified School District

J. Meghan McChesney
Colin P. Kelly Elementary School
Compton Unified School District

From Digging Dirt, to Shoveling Sh__

On another afternoon, when I got home from work, after I unlocked all my doors, I again checked the messages on my answering machine. Earlier in the day, Deirdre Thompson from the 4-H office left another message inviting me to become a member of the 4-H Program Development, Training, and Evaluation Committee. The committee's first meeting would be held in our school district's superintendent's office. And Dan Austin, one of the superintendent's aids, would be chairing the meeting.

Unfortunately, the meeting was going to be held during school hours, so that meant I would have to take time off from teaching to attend. Somewhat hesitantly, I called Deirdre back and agreed to go. What the heck, I figured; I had never been invited to be on a committee before. Plus, as Deirdre had hinted, I would be able to rub elbows with some pretty "important" people, in pretty "high" places.

Soon after I agreed, I received a letter from Dan Austin. The letter explained that the primary purpose of the committee was to establish guidelines for program quality; develop strategies for ongoing program evaluation; explore opportunities for research on youth-development issues; suggest and review curriculum directed at enhancing specific competencies and foundational skills for youth participants; coordinate with other youth-serving agencies; and develop resources and referrals for self-development

A few other important people were invited to be a part of the committee as well. There would be resident relations managers from the Housing Authority, VISTA program personnel, professors from various universities, elementary school principals, and a couple of directors from a research organization on the committee.

On the day of the big meeting up in the conference room of our school district's superintendent, I decided to take the day off from work. I had a bunch of sick days left to use up, so why not? The day before the meeting, I prepared enough work to help the substitute keep the kids busy, and then briefed the kids on the work that I had planned for them for the next day. They agreed that the work that I had left for them was a good idea, and promised to do as best they could to keep order in the room while I was gone.

I had no intentions of relying on the substitute for a productive day. In our large school district, you could never tell what kind of substitute you'd get from the large pool of subs available. And I knew my kids. If given the chance, some of them would rather mess around than keep busy with their learning.

The day of the meeting, I got up early, called the substitute desk, ordered a sub, and then called the school to let them know I wasn't coming in. Reason for absence: illness, of course.

Now, I could have stayed in bed and lounged around the house all morning, but I wanted to go over to the playground to check things out and, if they would let me, help the Housing Authority workers with some of the construction work. More than anything, I wanted to get down there, pick up a shovel, work up a sweat, and get a little dirty.

Back when I was putting myself through college, I worked construction for a few summers and loved the experience. I was an unskilled laborer, of course. I worked a jackhammer, shoveled gravel and sand, poured concrete, hauled concrete forms, tempered mortar for bricklayers, burned metal, picked up garbage—anything the foreman told me to do. Hard work, but good work. At the end of the day, I could look back on my work and know that I had accomplished something. Unlike teaching, everything was tangible. In teaching, even with all the testing and informal assessment, sometimes you never know if you're accomplishing anything.

My grandfather was a construction worker—a laborer, welder, boilermaker, and heavy equipment repairman. When I was little, he'd tell stories about his work over and over and over again. I can't tell you how many times I heard the story about digging the great tunnels in Chicago. Or the one about an explosion that nearly killed him and did kill the man standing right next to him. Or the one about this huge Native American who would run and jump from, or dive to, high beam to high beam on the skyscrapers that they helped to erect in Chicago. Once, after a long day of work, the "Indian," as Gramps liked to call him, jumped, missed, and fell to his death.

My brother, cousins, and I listened to Gramps tell his stories about a hundred times. I, for one, certainly never got bored, no matter how many times we'd hear his stories. He'd start off by saying, "Did I ever tell you about the time I . . ." and of course he had, about a thousand times before, but we never let him know. And he'd just tell us again and again and again. As a result, I always held a romantic view of construction, working with your hands and doing something with the material that Mother Earth so compassionately provided. For example, I had helped to design the playground that was emerging right there in Hacienda Village, but when I had worked on it before, it was on paper. What I really wanted to do then was to work with the real raw material. I wanted to dig dirt! And that's exactly what I got a chance to do.

When I got there, Jim Cole, Arthur Ammons, and Cruz Acuna were already hard at work. Jim and Arthur had recently been hired on to help with HACLA's modernization project. They both lived in Hacienda Village. Cruz, on the other hand, had been working with the Housing Authority for quite some time.

Talking with Cruz that morning as I began to work, I found out that his wife was a Special Education Teacher in my school district. That was a surprise. He really respected his wife's work.

That morning, the guys were busy spreading out the dirt that was recently dumped there to make for good ground for the sod that eventually would be planted. I grabbed a shovel and started right in. The foreman supervising the whole operation gave me a little bit of razzing for being there in the first place: "Hey, who's the new guy?" Somebody get 'im some gloves for those soft Jergen's hands. He's been pushing a pencil too long."

It felt good laboring again for a change. Oh sure, I would work up a sweat teaching in the stuffy classroom on a hot day, but this kind of work was something altogether different. Here, I could swear, burp, spit, and talk about sports, all in the same breath—every one of the stereotypical behaviors of true-blue construction work. I fit right in. Just like the old days.

After a couple of hours digging and smoothing out the dirt for the sod that would soon be coming, I had had enough. Guess I *had* been pushing a pencil too long. I wasn't in the shape I used to be. Besides, I had an excuse: It was lunch time and I had an important meeting to go to. So, I said good-bye to the guys, handed Jim my shovel, and took off towards home. Once I arrived, I quickly took off all my soiled clothes, jumped in the shower, ironed my shirt, put on my suit, helped myself to something to eat, and then climbed into my Jeep and drove to "The Hill" (what our school district's administrative offices are called, because they're located on Hill Street, in addition to being at the top of our hierarchical management ladder).

When I reached the administrative offices, all the invited committee members were already beginning to gather in the superintendent's conference room. Dan Austin greeted us at the door. What a voice on that man! Deep, resonating, and firm. His handshake reminded me of the guys hanging around Hacienda Village—slow, soft yet firm, with a lazy release. I liked it. And, I got a good impression of him.

Once everyone was settled, the first meeting of the new Program Development, Training, and Evaluation Committee of the Los Angeles 4-H After-School Activity Program got underway. We started with the usual introductions. Then we talked briefly about the purpose of the committee and heard a brief overview of current 4-H programs from John Pusey and Deirdre Thompson, 4-H Youth Development Advisors.

John and Deirdre, as expected, did a thorough job of explaining the various aspects of ongoing programs and the challenges they were facing. As I sat there listening I couldn't help but admire them both for their dedication, commitment, and effectiveness. John, in particular, sounded practically like a machine when talking. Precise.

After John and Deirdre were finished with the overview, I was ready to get right down to work. I certainly didn't want to get involved with the lengthy, arduous task of designing ourselves as a committee. To me, that seemed to be a total waste of time. I had definite ideas and I wanted to share them with the group. I wanted to begin right then and there, fulfilling my advisory role. But, that was not to be.

First, we heard from Sharon Hughes, who was co-chairing the meeting along with Dan Austin. Sharon, who worked in the resident relations department for the Housing Authority, shared with the group her perceptions of where the 4-H After-School Activity Program seemed to be heading. She felt that 4-H should steer more toward academics than anything else.

I almost went through the ceiling! No way! 4-H stands for head, hands, heart and health, not just head. If 4-H were to move more toward academics, then you might as well just tear off the other three leaves of the lucky 4-H four-leaf clover. No kid I knew wanted a one-leaf clover. All of a sudden, the purpose of 4-H was to make up for the public school system's incompetencies?

The public school system, according to its own short-sighted philosophy, was supposed to handle academics alone!

I vowed right then that as long as I was on that committee, I would provide a strong voice against a major emphasis on academics. If teachers couldn't accomplish the goals of the essentialistic framework of the public school system, then there was no reason why anyone else should attempt to. Let's just bore the kids to death with academics and basic skills for another three hours after school, why don't we?! And if the funding sources of 4-H were looking for improved standardized test scores, then, as far as I was concerned, they were missing the whole point of what 4-H stood for!

Now, don't get me wrong; I was all for academics, just not with the 4-H organization. Well, maybe, but only if the major umbrella of 4-H is labeled Community Service. Through community service, everything academic, hands-on, and health oriented could be accomplished. I thought 4-H, as developed through the university cooperative extension program, was supposed to show adults, through the successful efforts of children under university guidance, how to accomplish community objectives. Walk into a residents association meeting at one of the local Housing and Urban Development projects in your nearby inner city. Watch how the residents proceed with trying to accomplish anything. They're not very effective. Lots of potential, but certainly lacking a few skills.

Maybe, just maybe, it would be best to focus more on the task of teaching the children enrolled in the 4-H After-School Activity Program how to—as the 4-H Youth Development mission statement stated—"develop into responsible, self-directed, productive citizens of the world, and to improve the well-being of youth and society through the use of research-based learn-by-doing educational experiences." More academics wouldn't do that!

You won't find a better learn-by-doing educational experience than enabling youth to help improve or reconstruct the impoverished housing and urban developments that many of them lived within.

Planting Our Playground

We had to fight hard to get the opportunity, but eventually we were allowed to complete the landscape design of the playground. It appeared as though the construction managers didn't want us to be involved at first, but because Meghan and I were so persistent, they finally conceded that the kids could complete the landscaping. The construction supervisor gave us a large catalogue, which provided pictures and descriptions of thousands of different plants from which we could choose. And the housing authority appropriated $1,200 for any combination of plants the kids wanted to buy.

Meghan and I talked about it and decided that she, Darin, and another young boy, named Christopher, who was also very helpful with the original architectural plans, would look through the catalogue and pick out the plants that were most appropriate for completing the landscape design. The rest of the 4-H'ers would go with me to the playground to dig eighteen holes for our raised rose garden.

In addition to the plants that we would receive from the Housing Authority, we were also going to be receiving eighteen bare-root rose bushes for our garden! Don MacNeil, the Metro Coordinator from the 4-H office was able to arrange for John Walden, from Jackson & Perkins Roses, to donate the bushes.

During the time that Meghan and I were making arrangements with 4-H to begin the process of drawing up the landscape design and dig the eighteen holes, Darin unexpectedly received a very important letter. The letter came directly to the school. The return address on the manila envelope said it was from the U. S. Department of Housing and Urban Development! I knew it had to be important, so at lunch, I pulled Darin off the playground and brought him to the office so that he could open the letter in the presence of our principal.

When Darin opened the letter, he knew right away who it was from. Proudly, he read the letter to us:

> Dear Darin:
>
> I am pleased and honored to have this opportunity to send my personal greeting and thanks to you for your contribution to the 'Caution: Children At Work!' program. You have demonstrated a remarkable commitment to improve yourself and the community. You are part of an exemplary educational and civic partnership which inspires and motivates students to succeed in life. Our nation needs your talents and I wish you all the best of luck in everything you do.
>
> Sincerely, Henry Cisneros

At the end of the letter, in his personal handwriting, Mr. Cisneros also wrote Darin a note:

> I enjoyed meeting you in Washington and want to encourage you in your community involvements. We need all your talents for the future of our country.

A few days later, we began the landscaping phase of our project. While Darin stayed inside with Meghan and Christopher to design the landscaping, with shovels in hand, I led the remaining 4-H'ers out to the playground and began measuring and digging the eighteen holes for the rose bushes. We planned to have the holes dug according to the exact quantifiable specifications that Mr. Walden provided. We were required to measure the depth and diameter of the holes, and the distance between them as well—a pretty good math lesson for the kids, I thought.

When we finally started digging, dirt was everywhere. Dry dirt, muddy dirt, sloppy dirt—you name it. They were such good little diggers.

In retrospect, I realize how I could have used this opportunity to introduce the kids to the idea that the holes they were digging were somehow embedded in the ground of our own being—the natural, living, regenerating organism we call Earth. I could've tried to awaken them to the thought that we are all born of the Earth and are intimately connected to it. I could've helped them to realize that the Earth brings us life as surely as does the blood flowing through our veins. I should've helped them to realize that the world and the universe around it are not just some mass of material, some resource that we could use, dominate, manipulate, and exploit for our own selfish aims. It was not some clocklike machine of juxtaposed parts devoid of spirit, ordered by mathematical and quantifiable laws.

But, such was not the case. I wasn't moving slowly enough to be that insightful. And I wasn't quite that aware of all the implications and manifestations of my newly formed holistic or ecological worldview. Besides, it wasn't a part of our original plan. Instead, that first day, we concentrated on working hard enough to get all the holes started. And when it was time to go, I left knowing that most of the work was already done. In my compulsive way, I was only too glad to know that we were nearing the completion of a task. And the next day, while school was still in session, and my brain was intent on finishing the job, I took the kids in my classroom out to the playground to culminate the digging of the holes.

Soon thereafter, when all the holes were dug for the rose bushes, Darin received yet another unexpected letter. The return address on the manila envelope this time read, "The White House." When Darin read this letter, he did so during the 4-H After-School Program in presence of all the other 4-H'ers and a reporter from the *Los Angeles Times.*

He opened up the envelope slowly and carefully, with an ever-widening grin on his bright young face. Then, also slowly and carefully, as if to fully savor the moment, he read the letter. Basically the letter thanked the group for the project and the example it set in how schoolchildren can make a difference. Then, after pausing for effect, Darin read:

> Young people like you represent the future of our nation. . . . Best wishes for a wonderful new year.
>
> Sincerely, Bill Clinton

After Darin finished reading the letter and we offered our congratulations, he once again slowly and carefully folded it up, looked at us with his glistening eyes, and said, "See?! This is what kids can do!" Feeling like a kid myself, filled with the joy of being vicariously acknowledged by the President of the United States of America, I knew Darin was right—this is what we can do!

With a newfound sense of excitement and importance about what we were doing, we gathered everyone up, grabbed all of our gardening tools, and set off in the direction of the playground in Hacienda Village Housing Development.

That day, Mr. Walden brought a wonderful combination of rose bushes with him to the playground for all of us to plant. He treated us to six of his "Ingrid Bergmans," which were dark red, fully double blooming roses with a texture like fine velvet. He also had six "Sun Flares," which, we were told, would carry loads of yellow, low-growing blooms that would habitually spread out when they began to grow. And he brought six of my favorite, which he called his "Baby Blanket" roses. These rose bushes were said to be tough as nails and extremely disease resistant. This would be a good thing, we thought, because any rose bush that went into our playground would have to be tough, for there would always be a lot of reckless kids playing there.

Mr. Walden did a great job of teaching the kids how to plant the bushes, and of course the kids did a fabulous job of planting them. After we finished planting the eighteen rose bushes, a few of the kids were given the opportunity to water them down. Mr. Walden instructed that the rose bushes had to be embedded in a very soupy like bowl of mud and water if they were going to take. So the kids poured on the water.

As all the adults present helped the kids complete their work, I took the opportunity to stand back to watch how wonderful things were turning out. It was easy to imagine how things would look when the roses finally started to bloom. I could hardly wait. The playground was at last nearing completion.

When the watering of all the rose bushes was completed, we all lugged our shovels back to school and were treated by a presentation from Meghan, Darin, and Christopher. They had completed the landscape design. When they showed us their plans, it was agreed that they had done an excellent job.

The following day, Meghan and I took the plans to the construction manager so that he could order the plants. He, too, was impressed with the kids' design. Surprisingly, a few days later, when the plants arrived, Meghan and I had to fight once again to convince the construction crew to leave a few flowers, bushes, and trees for the 4-H'ers and my class to plant. I couldn't believe it. Why we had to fight for the opportunity to plant everything, I would never know. The construction managers *were* getting tired of us by that time, but I didn't care. As far as I was concerned, the kids needed the experience. Why the construction crew couldn't see that, I'll never know.

The construction crew finally agreed to leave a bunch of bushes and flowers on the sidewalk so that we could come back the next day to plant them. The next day, during school hours, I took my class out to the playground, with a few of the plants we had also planted in the small patch of dirt next to our classroom, to begin the job. And, of course, after school, Meghan and I took all the 4-H'ers to the playground to finish the planting.

After the 4-H'ers chose their particular planting tasks, one of the local residents of Hacienda Village, a fiery little woman named Connie, came by to help. I had met Connie earlier at one of the residents' meetings that I first attended back when Meghan and I had originally inquired about the possibility of renovating the playground. And then once when the construction of the playground had been underway, I brought her over to show off the work that the 4-H'ers had done. It was then that I kiddingly started calling her "Granny." She didn't like it at first, but I only did it because she had been calling me "Johnny." I figured she had it coming. Nobody called me Johnny. Sometimes, Meghan would call me John-John, but I didn't mind that. I kind of liked it, actually. Besides, Meghan could call me anything, and I wouldn't mind.

So when Granny—or rather Connie—arrived at the playground and saw us planting, she came over and started yelling at me for not telling her beforehand. I wasn't aware of it, but apparently she had wanted to be involved with the planting. Clearly, planting was something that she enjoyed. After Connie finished yelling, and after I completed my apologizing, she got down on her hands and knees and started digging in the dirt. She turned out to be a great help, too. A regular landscaping forewoman! She told all the 4-H'ers what to do and prodded a few other neighborhood kids, who were sitting around watching, to get off their duffs and help out. She even got a couple of kids from the Boys and Girls Club to come over and lend a hand.

The playground, and the planting, turned out to be real community affair right up until the last moment.

The Dedication

On the day of the final dedication of our playground, I was practically dead. Dead-tired, exhausted. It was only the day before, with Connie's help, that we were barely able to finish all the planting in time. After all the 4-H'ers had left, Meghan, Connie, and I stayed on until 8:00 PM making sure that everything was in order, that all the plants were firmly in the ground. And during the days that we were completing the landscaping design, planting the rose bushes and the remaining plants that the housing authority ordered for us, we also had to prepare all the kids for their final presentation at the dedication. Whew! It was a lot more work than any of us had anticipated.

On the day of the dedication, Meghan and I took the day off from work. Luckily for me, Mrs. Ruiz arranged to have a substitute handle my class for the day. I was grateful because this allowed me the opportunity to work with Meghan to get everything ready for the big event. All the kids from my class would attend the dedication, because, after all, they were the ones that got the whole project started, but now a substitute would be there to watch them while I took care of the logistics.

Meghan and I spent a lot of time beforehand preparing all the kids, getting them ready, rehearsing for the big day. Darin was due to be our shining star, same as before, when he presented the architectural designs. Actually, he was going to "co-MC" the event along with Don Smith, the Executive Director of the Housing Authority. Christopher, the young man who was like Darin's assistant, would also help to explain all of the architectural and landscaping designs to the people in the audience. And a bright little girl, Shaneka, would lead the rest of the 4-H'ers in the reciting of the 4-H pledge.

We were expecting quite an audience to be there. The week before, Meghan and I raked through Hacienda Village, passing out invitations. And the public relations staff from the Housing Authority invited all kinds of dignitaries to the big event. The only drawback to this was the fact that we had to work the big event around councilman Rudy Svorinich's schedule. Apparently, the most important person at the dedication would be Mr. Svorinich—a person who had nothing to do with the playground at all. Idealistically, the schedule probably should've worked around the kids' availability—they had everything to do with the playground!

So, anyway, before Meghan and I took the whole crowd of 4-H'ers over to the playground, we had them gather in the 4-H room at our school. They all looked fantastic. Just as we had asked, they were well dressed for the occasion. All the girls were wearing pretty dresses and most of the boys were wearing suits. Darin, as expected, donned his double-breasted. Personally, I would've preferred they arrive in T-shirts, shorts, and sneakers. We were, after all, dedicating a playground.

After all the kids were gathered, and after Meghan and I were sure they knew exactly what to do and how to behave, we walked over to the playground in single-file fashion. You should have seen them parading over to the playground. Everyone in Hacienda noticed how handsome they all looked.

When we arrived, all the adults, dignitaries, and press were still mingling and getting ready to settle down. Looking around to see who was there from the community, I was glad to see that Connie made it for the event. Victor was hanging around in the back as usual. My classroom of kids was there. And I could see that the construction crew was also at hand—Jim, Dee, Cruz, Arthur, and the rest.

Don Smith, and of course Darin, the two co-MC's got the event underway. Mr. Smith thanked everyone for coming, acknowledged the special dignitaries that were present and then turned over the microphone to Darin. Darin promptly introduced our 4-H'ers, and they in turn invited the audience to stand so that we could pledge allegiance to our country. After that, the 4-H'ers recited their little 4-H pledge.

With the pledges completed, Richard Linsey, president of the Hacienda Village resident's association, began the round of talks from the dignitaries.

The local councilman, Rudy Svorinich, pretty much concluded the speech giving that early afternoon.

After that, the kids, led by Meghan, once again explained their design. Then the big ribbon-cutting ceremony began. Rudy, the most important person there, the guy who had nothing to do with the development of the playground, held the scissors, of course. And all of the other dignitaries from the Housing Authority and the Mayor's office elbowed their way in to hold the ribbon. Little Darin got in there, too. Meghan and I watched from a distance.

When the ribbon cutting was over, and the press had taken all their pictures, the kids jumped on all the equipment and played for a long, long time. Meghan took pictures of all the kids, dressed in their suits and dresses, climbing all over everything. I spent much of my time talking with the residents.

After everyone had left, Meghan and I stayed around to clean up the entire area. We put the architectural boards back into Meghan's car, returned the school's PA system back to its proper place, and then went home. I then took off my suit, crawled into bed, and promptly passed out.

An Angel and a Pearl

Sometime later, after another particularly difficult week at work, I trudged home feeling tired and down. After reaching my house, I unlocked all the locks, opened my bedroom door, and flopped down on the bed. When I awoke, it was dark outside. I got up, and opened up my bedroom door to view Meghan relaxing on the sofa in the living room. She was watching a video.

I didn't want to be around any noise, so I decided to take a nice, calm, leisurely walk around the neighborhood to shake off all the crud that had climbed on my back from another exhausting week of work. Briefly explaining to Meghan that I needed to take a walk, I reached for the door and bolted outside.

Wiping the sleep from my eyes, I slowly stumbled towards Hacienda Village. It was quiet out and the night air was warm. A good night for a walk—or so I thought. When I was about midway past Hacienda Village, three boys shouting, "Mr. Guuust," came running after me. Waking up quickly, I started running in the opposite direction. I had had enough of children from the week, so I certainly didn't want a bunch of sweaty, stinky kids chasing after me. All I wanted to do was to take a nice quiet walk to stretch my legs and do some thinking.

While dodging around the corner of a unit in Hacienda Village to get away from the charging kids, a woman sitting in her porch rocking chair, who must have seen everything, yelled out, "Hey, leave that man alone. Can't you see he doesn't want to be bothered?"

Luckily for me, her yelling worked. The three boys stopped dead in their tracks, turned, and walked back to where they had been playing.

I thanked her profusely for what she had done, and continued walking. But much to my surprise, she wouldn't let me, "Hey, come back here. Who are you? What are you doing around here? I know you. You're that teacher, aren't you? What are you doing around here? Come here."

Sighing heavily, I walked up to the porch where she was sitting, listening to music, smoking cigarettes, sipping on her booze. I sat down on the hard concrete across from her, reached my hand out to shake hers, and said, "Hi, my name's John. And yeah, I'm a teacher at the elementary school over on 104th Street."

"Name's Rochelle," she answered back with a slur. She obviously had been sitting there for a while.

After our introductions, she started asking questions: "What are you doing livin' in this neighborhood? You part Black or something? You like Blacks especially? You single or married?"

Of course, I had to explain to her that I was living here in the neighborhood because I thought it was the right thing to do. That, to the best of my knowledge, I didn't have any Black ancestry, and didn't have any more liking for Black people than I did for any other group of people. I didn't tell her whether I was single or married, though.

When she was satisfied with my straight answers, she became a little more comfortable with who I was. In turn, I also became a little more comfortable with just hanging around, relaxing and enjoying the warm night. Curiously, I didn't feel the need to get up to do anymore walking or being alone to think.

Slowly, we started talking about just about everything. You know, nothing in particular, everything in general. Once in a while, while we were talking, she'd hush me, turn her music up real loud, and start swaying with it. She'd say, "Shhh, this is my song. Skuse me." Somewhat amused, I obediently did as she asked and sat there on the cool concrete, watching.

After sitting there quietly for a while, Rochelle asked, "You want to go with me to the liquor store to get another bottle?"

"Sure. Why not," I said.

While Rochelle went inside to get some money, I got up and brushed myself off. When she returned, we began walking through Hacienda Village towards Compton Avenue. There were a lot of people out, so, naturally, we attracted a lot of looks. Nobody said anything directly to us, but we could hear the snickering as we walked. When we reached the liquor store, I went inside but didn't look to see what kind of booze she was buying, but I knew it was the hard kind. Stuff I never drank.

Returning to her porch, I sat back down on the concrete and tried my best to listen to Rochelle as she kept talking. Most of the time, however, I was mesmerized by the three boys playing nearby under the bulletproof lights. I heard most of what Rochelle was saying, and I did keep the conversation flowing, but at the same time, something unusual began to happen. It was as if time started standing still. Everything became louder, brighter, clearer, more significant, luminous.

It was actually a glorious moment. The lights were shining down on the three boys, and the glistening grass, which was becoming damp from the nighttime air, flickered and sparkled below their dirty little bare feet. In the background, out towards the street, it was dark, but the outlines of trees and cars could vaguely be seen.

Just then, as everything was standing still, the smallest of the three boys silently ran up to me, grabbed my wrist, placed a tiny pearl in my outstretched hand, and quickly scurried off without saying a word. Looking down to take a closer look at the pearl, I realized that he must have gotten it off of some cheap plastic toy necklace or something. Still, I was amazed. Why did he do that just then?

When I looked up, the biggest boy had one knee on the ground and the other two boys, while pretending that their forefingers were attached to the big boy's head, began running, skipping, and dancing in circles around him. When they all started to sing and hum, I was reminded of a miniature carousel at a carnival.

Sitting there, listening to Rochelle's music, watching her continue to rock, I began rolling the little pearl around in my hand. After showing Rochelle the pearl that the little boy gave me, I asked her, "Who are those three boys?"

"The big one kneeling down," she started, "is my son. His name is Damion. The other older boy is Alfredo. And the little one who just put that pearl in your hand is Angel."

For the first time since moving into the neighborhood, everything was perfect. I didn't have to fix anything, didn't have to make anything better, didn't have any ideal to manifest. The school year was finally coming to a close, all of our social action projects were completed, all of our democratic struggles in the classroom were over, all my fighting with the system was at an end. Everything—if only for that brief moment—was exactly as I needed it to be. Exhausted but totally relaxed, I felt content, happy, free. Realizing that this sense of happiness and freedom came from nowhere else other than my own sense of calm and stillness, that it had nothing at all to do with any emancipating or liberating efforts directed towards the outside world, I had nothing left to do other than sit there with Angel's pearl in my hand, under the glow of the bulletproof lights . . . and be.